FINDING MR. RIGHT

A Woman's Guide To Meeting Men

AMERICA'S #1 SINGLES EXPERT

DON DIEBEL

gemini publishing
Houston, Texas

Copyright © 1990

By Don Diebel

GEMINI PUBLISHING COMPANY
11543 Gullwood Drive
Houston, TX 77089

ALL RIGHTS RESERVED

No part of this book may be reproduced by any mechanical, photographic, or electronic process, or in the form of a phonographic recording, nor may it be stored in an information retrieval system, transmitted, or otherwise be copied for public or private use without the written permission of the publisher.

Library of Congress No. 89-80150
ISBN 0-937164-02-X

Publishers Cataloging in Publication Data
Diebel, Don R., 1947-
Finding Mr. right.
Includes index.
1. Single people. 2. Interpersonal relations.
1. Title
HQ800.   301.4   89-80150

CONTENTS

1. Meeting Men in Nightclubs..................9

How to select a good nightclub. The 14 different types of men you will encounter in nightclubs. What to wear. Getting ready and psyched up. Drugs. Nightclub "Hot Spots." Flirting. How to approach a man. Fast-dancing. Slow-dancing.

* **Exclusive Interviews With Single Men**..................33

2. Where to Meet Men..................39

The hitchhiker. Parties. Daytime Barfly. Volunteer activities. Hotels and motels. Parks. The supermarket. Tennis. Rafting. Trips. Jogging. Roller Rinks. Art Galleries. Skiing. Department stores. Restaurants. Transportation. Churches. Human Potential groups. Health clubs. Swimming pools. Tours. Theater groups. Friends and relatives. At work. The beach. Adult education and university extension courses. Male strip joints. Nudist parks, clubs, beaches, and resorts.

3. Dating Services..................65

Computer dating. Dating referral services. Video dating.

4. How to Meet Men Using Personal Ads..................71

How to get men to write to you first. When the man answers your ad. Your letter. You write the men first. Magazines with free pen pal columns and pen pal clubs.

CONTENTS

5. Singles Vacations..100

> Club Med. Singleworld cruises. Singleworld land vacations. Windjammer Barefoot cruises.

6. How and Where to Meet Wealthy Men...................107

> What to wear. Places where wealthy men hang out. Occupations where you will meet wealthy men. Gaining the necessary exposure.

7. How to Meet Male Flight Attendants....................112

> Why flight attendants are ideal for a warm, mature, and completely sexual affair. How to approach him in the air. Where to meet them on the ground. How to pick them up.

8. Unique Ways to Meet Men....................................116

> The circular method. The book method. The card method.

9. How to Talk to a Man...120

> Things to talk about. The secret to getting a man to fall in love with you. How to spice up your conversation. The aggressive approach that turns men off. Touching while talking. Voice tone.

10. Body Language...123

> How to use body language to attract men. How to recognize male body language that says he is available. How to recognize male

CONTENTS

body language that means he's interested in you. How to recognize his negative body language.

11. Looks 127

Why women do not have to be beautiful to attract men. Your hair. Jewelry. Obesity. Good grooming. Hold your liquor.

12. For Shy Women Only 129

Shyness defined. Disadvantages of being shy. Misconceived beliefs of shy women. How to overcome shyness at nightclubs. Overcoming shyness using subliminal tapes.

13. How to Meet Men Using Astrology 143

How to do his horoscope. Using astrology to pick up men at nightclubs. Seduction routine.

14. How to Meet Men Using the Powers of the Mind ... 145

How to meet men using self-hypnosis. Alternate method of self-hypnosis. How to meet men using a hypnotic sleep tape. How to meet men using autosuggestion. The mirror technique for meeting men. Using mental pictures to meet men. How to use mental telepathy to meet men.

15. 10 Cities With the Most Available Single Men 168

  * **Special Bonus Section (100 Ways to Meet and Attract Men) 171**

INTRODUCTION

You've heard the old saying, "a good man is hard to find."

This book offers proven and practical solutions for the overwhelming number of women who face the very real problem of finding a good man or as I like to call him, "Mr. Right."

I wrote this book on the basis of three underlying principles:

First, using the law of probabilities. If you make it your goal to constantly go where and be where many men congregate, and if you put all your efforts into trying to meet and go out with as many men as possible, you will sooner or later meet a man who will fulfill all your dreams. A man capable of intimacy, not afraid of commitment, communicates, and will fall in love with you exactly as you are.

As you read, "Finding Mr. Right," you're going to be amazed at the many ways and techniques to meet men.

Try as many methods as possible. Don't put all your eggs in one basket. A good example of this are women who only go to nightclubs to meet men. Date <u>many</u> men and date often! Set a goal to meet and go out with a hundred men. Long before you have met your one hundredth man, in most cases, you will have found at least one, but more probably, <u>many</u> men who will be right for you.

To sum it up, you need exposure and visibility. One of the major reasons you may not be finding Mr. Right is simply because you're not meeting enough men.

The second principle is based upon man's inability to make the first move because of shyness and fear of rejection.

This book will teach you to go after what you want and be-

INTRODUCTION

come aggressive. Believe me, men want you to make the first move.

Today the choice is all yours. Either you can sit around waiting for men to approach you...or use the surefire techniques in this book to take control of your love-life once and for all.

Women have no idea how much power they have over men. It's always been the woman who said yes or no and allowed the relationship to start.

Now, after reading this book you can actually go up to the man, let him know you're interested in him and have exactly the kind of relationship you're looking for. Your social power becomes almost limitless.

You've got to take action to get the things you want out of life! Don't sit around waiting for your "knight in shining armor" to come into your life. If you leave the business of finding love with the right man to chance, chances are it will pass you by.

Sure, this is going to involve some risk-taking and courage to be aggressive in meeting men. With practice, it will come natural and besides, this is an investment in your future with "Mr. Right."

The last principle this book is based on, is using the powers of the subconscious mind to meet men and reprogram your mind with positive thoughts and eliminate the negative "garbage" in your subconscious mind that causes you problems with the opposite sex.

You may be a little skeptical of some of these methods to reprogram your mind to meet men, overcome shyness, gain confidence with men, etc. These proven scientific methods are guaranteed to work and will work for you if you back them with desire and belief. With practice, you will be meeting more men than you ever dreamed possible!

In closing, make finding "Mr. Right" your top priority in life. Set goals and become obsessed with attracting him.

I've designed a personal game plan for you to find "Mr. Right" that works. The rest is up to you. *Happy Hunting!*

CHAPTER ONE

Meeting Men in Nightclubs

Where's one of the best places in your city to attract or meet a man? You guessed it right. A club. This is where men go to unwind and release their pent-up pressures and emotions, not to mention, meeting a girl like yourself. The clubs provide an atmosphere of sensual stimulation with all the music, lights, pulsating rhythms, and the erotic and exotic motions of dancers.

There's and art to meeting a man in a club and this book will lead you and guide you from the moment you walk in the door until the time you leave. You will learn how to approach the nightclub man and what to do after you have made contact.

If you're a shy woman, reading this book will give you the confidence and the ability to meet men at the clubs. Using the methods employed in this book, your fear of the opposite sex will disappear and you won't be standing on the sidelines anymore watching the other women meet men.

You may be a little skeptical of some of the methods used in to meet men in this book. These methods will work for any woman that employs them backed with desire and belief. If you don't believe they will work for you, just try them out for yourself and you will be amazed at the results. With practice, you will be meeting more men than you ever dreamed possible.

Let's not waste anymore time talking about what you're going to learn and get down to business and "make it" with the nightclub man.

How to Select a Good Club

When selecting a club, you want to select one where most of the men are. To do this, you can try and hit as many clubs as possible and check out the action for yourself or you can ask your friends that frequent the nightclub scene. However, what they consider a great place to meet men may not necessarily be the best place to go. You might also ask the door man upon arriving, what's the best night for action. Also, while you're there, inquire if they have a ladies night when ladies drink free or get a discount on their drinks. These specials attract men to clubs like crazy!

When shopping around for a club, don't make the fatal mistake of judging a club on the basis of one night. Certain nights can just be an off night. This is normal and happens at all clubs.

Don't waste your time going to a club where there's mostly women. The more men there are, the chances are greatly increased of you meeting someone.

You may want to select an exclusive membership club if you can afford it. Just make it a point to take an introductory tour. Sometimes it's free or you pay a cover charge to check it out.

Conventional clubs are just as good, if not better. The majority of people might not be upperclass and rich but this will be to your advantage and I will explain why. An upperclass, high society jet-setter nightclub man is usually narcissistic and self-centered and if you don't have money you're just scum of the earth. There are exceptions to the rule but perhaps not very many.

Your conventional club is your best bet in my opinion. Here you will find a variety of men, the rich and barely-making-it, the construction worker, the handsome man, the engineer, the cute

Meeting Men in Nightclubs

man, and your average Joe. They all have the same thing in common and that is to get out on that dance floor and shed their inhibitions and most important of all, to meet a nice, sweet woman like yourself.

In conclusion, find a nightclub where the greatest number of men are and that you feel comfortable in and keep going there as often as possible. Make an effort to meet as many people as possible, including other women. Afterall, women know guys and they can introduce you to their male friends. By going to this place often, you will become a familiar face and you will be amazed at the number of friends and acquaintances you will make. So get out there and make the rounds and find yourself a good nightclub. Just keep going to this nightclub and see if your social life doesn't improve dramatically.

Also, I might add, don't just go to a few nightclubs when selecting a nightclub. Go to all of them so you can make a good comparison as to which ones are the best. Some nightclubs are good only on a particular night. Find out what night that is and make an effort to be there every week.

I know you have heard various comments in books, media, etc. about nightclubs being one of the worst places to look for a relationship or a husband. A lot of my female friends have met real nice men and had satisfying relationships with men they have met in nightclubs.

So, don't rule out nightclubs as good place to meet men. Try several different methods of meeting men. Don't put all your eggs in one basket and use nightclubs solely for the purpose of meeting the opposite sex.

I hear complaints from women saying, "There just aren't any good men around anymore." Believe me, they are in nightclubs too. You just have to look for them and weed out the bad ones.

Some women make the fatal mistake of carrying a negative attitude with them when they go to nightclubs. They think that all the guys there are just a bunch of jerks and out for just one thing and that's sex. This attitude can prevent you from meeting someone really nice. There are some really nice men in nightclubs that will treat you with respect.

FINDING MR. RIGHT

The Nightclub Man

I will describe the different types of men you will encounter at the nightclubs.

First, I will begin with the undesirable types which should be avoided if at all possible, because you will just be wasting your time. Believe me, you don't want to waste your precious time trying to meet a man you're not going to get anywhere with. Before you know it, closing time will creep upon you and you will say to yourself, "I wasted my whole damn night on that jerk and here I am going home alone without at least giving some real nice guy my phone number tonight."

The following are what I classify as the undesirable types:

The Woman Hater

Why in the hell these men go to nightclubs I'll never be able to figure out. Because of some negative experiences with the opposite sex and because they have been hurt, they think all women are bitches. These men will just sit there with a stone face, rejecting any glances from the opposite sex. If you approach them and try to start up a conversation, they give you a go to hell look that says, "Go away bitch."

No matter what approach you use, how beautiful you are, or how friendly you act, you will be rejected. A lot of these men subconsciously gain immense pleasure our of putting women down. Some will even tell you to go to hell or get lost if you ask them to dance or just by trying to start up a conversation with them.

I'm just glad this type of put down does not happen very often. Usually, men do not object to a woman approaching them.

If you run into this type of man, whatever you do, DON'T try to get even with him by putting him down and showing anger towards him. He loves that and there is nothing he would like better than to see you get bent out of shape. By making you

Meeting Men in Nightclubs

unhappy, it makes him happy to see females suffer. Simply ignore his rejection towards you and move on to the next available man. Fortunately, you will not run into many men like this. There's plenty of men who want to meet and mingle with the opposite sex.

The Teaser

Unfortunately you will run into these types at the nightclubs and in all areas of life. You have seen them in high school, college, at work, male strip joints, etc. Just learn to recognize them and ignore and avoid them. I will give you some tips on how to spot them:

1. He wears very revealing clothes. He wears very tight clothes, also. The non-teaser wears these kind of clothes to attract females attention, but the teaser wears them with the attitude of, "You can look but you better not touch." The minute you try to get physical with him or try to make advances toward him, he gives you the big brush off. Showing off his body is just to attract attention and nothing else.

2. While dancing he's looking like male strippers, thrusting his hips back and forth and shaking his crotch at you. He's doing this on purpose to turn you on and fool you into thinking he's and easy catch. The song ends and he says, "Thank you" and disappears into the crowd. Before you know it he's back up on the dance floor with another woman doing the same thing to her. He will do this with several women, never spending much time with any particular woman. He gets his thrills by turning on as many females as possible on the dance floor, but has no intentions whatsoever of getting picked up or meeting anyone.

3. Here's one that really bothers you. You see this really handsome man flirting with you and really giving you the eye. You try to meet this man and he tells you, "I've got to go to the restroom" and then he never returns. Another one is, "I've got to go look for my friend" and never returns. Later you see him in another part of the nightclub. He deliberately leaves the

FINDING MR. RIGHT

scene to avoid making any contact with any woman, much less you.

4. This will really frustrate you. You ask this guy to slow dance and he accepts. Your bodies meet and he starts grinding his crotch into yours. You're getting turned on and horny. All this time you're thinking he's horny too and wants to make love to you. The song ends and he abruptly breaks away and says, "Thank you" then disappears into the crowd. Then you say in your mind, "That damned teasing bastard!"

5. This is known as a big flirt. He walks around flirting with every woman in sight. When a woman approaches him trying to make contact, he rejects her advances or makes up an excuse to leave the scene.

6. This experience can really blow your mind. You meet a man and you drink and dance the night away. You think you're really hitting it off good together and you get the impression he will go home with you or at least ask for your phone number. You ask him if he would like to come over to your place for awhile. He says, "No" and you ask him if he would like to leave and get a bite to eat at a local restaurant. He still says, "No." So you say, "Well can I give you a call sometime?" He replies, "I don't give out my phone number to strangers." So it ends up that you wasted your whole night on this one man.

The Drinkaholic

This is a man who uses women to support a drinking habit. He may even come right out and ask you, "Would you buy me a drink?" upon meeting you. Most women will say no and would be rather offended. After he finishes his drink he will say, "Can I have another drink?" One drink leads to another and before you know it, you have dished out a lot of money on his drinks.

This all can sure be to your advantage or disadvantage. On the positive side, he may go home with you in exchange for buying him drinks. He may get so drunk it may be necessary to take him home and put him to bed. Of course on the negative side he may just use you to buy him drinks and then blow you

Meeting Men in Nightclubs

off and leave the nightclub or even move on to the next fool who will buy him drinks.

In conclusion, use your better judgement before you start dishing out a lot of money on buying a man drinks. You could be taken for a ride. Fortunately, you will very rarely run into this type of man.

The (Dance Only) Man

This is the man that goes to the nightclub to dance only. He's not going there to be hustled, attract women or go home with anybody. He just wants to dance and have a good time.

In some cases he might be married or going out on his girlfriend. This would explain why he would just want to dance, with no strings attached, that is if he wants to remain faithful.

Although this type may be undesirable initially because of his reluctance to be approached, don't give up on him. The next night you see him, dance with him again as many times as possible. After you practically become dancing partners, you will become more and more acquainted with each other and before you know it he will have other things on his mind besides dancing.

Out With The Boys Night

These are groups of men who come to the nightclubs to socialize among themselves. They may be all single, married, or both. They came to the nightclub to have a few drinks and shoot the bull. Some just want to socialize among themselves and don't want to be bothered by any females.

It's rather difficult to meet men who are in a group like this, much less make contact. Some of them may dance, but after the dance they go rushing back to their male friends and just ignore you. If you can determine a man is part of a group like his and he ignores you and seems like he's just interested in his friends, don't waste your time and move on to greener pastures.

If you find out he's married and with a group of married

FINDING MR. RIGHT

men, you're really at a dead end street. They should not even be there in the first place. I strongly recommend not having anything to do with a married man at a nightclub. What if his wife walks in the nightclub and sees her husband with another woman? This can only spell trouble. Let me warn you and take my advice, STAY AWAY FROM MARRIED MEN!

Golddigger

This man is mainly interested in how much material wealth and money you have. Upon meeting you, he will ask personal questions like, "What do you do for a living?", "How much money do you make?", "What kind of car do you drive?", "Do you own your own home?", or "Do you have a boat?"

If you're not a woman of financial means, he won't have anything to do with you. He will consider you too low-classed to associate with. If you are a woman of financial means, then you will probably hit it off real well with this type of man. This can have its drawbacks though, because he may just like you for your money and not for yourself.

This concludes the undesirable types. Now I will describe the desirable types you will encounter at the nightclubs:

The Woman-Hunter

This man goes to nightclubs with one purpose in mind. To meet women and get approached by you. This is one of the easiest types to meet because there are no hassles involved. You meet, have a couple drinks and dance, and he's ready and willing to go home with you. He may come right out and tell you, "I want to make love to you" or "Lets leave and go to your place." An aggressive man may scare some women off but don't let it bother you. Admire a man having courage to go for what he wants.

Some of these men are very active sexually and like to play musical sex partners. They need sex constantly and with a variety of sexual partners. It's nice to meet a man like this sometimes, but most likely it will turn into a one-nighter. He wakes up the next day and gets dressed and walks right out of your life.

One possible drawback from meeting a sexually active man like this is contracting a social disease. Of course, how are you supposed to know he has been sleeping with every Mary, Jane, and Linda in the city. You just have to be careful who you sleep with these days.

These types are usually easy to spot. They actively flirt and smile at the opposite sex and are extremely friendly. They will just stand around the dance floor where they encourage females to ask them to dance. They of course, may ask you to dance. I really admire a man who takes the initiative to ask a woman to dance. Some men are so shy about asking a woman to dance in the first place.

Also, I might add, these men usually come to the nightclubs alone. However, they come with a male friend occasionally. A man alone will get approached more often by females. So, for the Woman-Hunter, it's really an advantage for him to go to the nightclubs alone so he will be approached more frequently.

The High and Loaded Man

This is a man who is either high on liquor or drugs or even both. After a few drinks or under the influence of drugs, he will be feeling rather loose and perhaps even horny. Naturally, this is to your advantage because it makes your prey easier to catch.

How do you spot this man? By simple observation. His walk will be unsteady, while perhaps bumping into people while he is walking. If he has been drinking heavily, he will make several trips to the restroom. By standing next to the mens restroom, you can observe who's going back and forth to the restroom. An exception to this is a man that has a kidney or bladder problem.

If he's under the influence of drugs, his pupils will be very large. If he's loaded on downers, he will walk as if he were drunk and his speech will be somewhat slurred.

Don't come on real strong and act real aggressive with this

FINDING MR. RIGHT

man. He possibly may think that you are trying to take advantage of him because he's loaded. Just be nice and gentle with him.

The Mate-Seeker

This is a man who is actively seeking a lover or girlfriend. He's unattached and looking for a relationship. Perhaps in the back of his mind he's wanting to settle down and get married.

Unfortunately, a nightclub is not the best place in the world to look for a long-term relationship or marriage partner. A lot of men are just out to see how many different women they can make love to and don't want to be tied down to any serious relationships. They have a love them and leave them attitude. The same thing applies to some women who frequent nightclubs.

This type of man is highly desirable because he's very friendly and easy to make contact with. You can make a very strong impression on this man by showing him that you're interested in him and care for him. You shouldn't have any problem getting him to leave to get something to eat or go home with you, if you play your cards right.

The Rich Man

He is usually dressed in expensive clothes and perhaps wears a lot of gold and diamonds. He may be a bit on the snobbish side because he thinks he's better than everyone else. If you are on the same level as this man and well-to-do yourself, you will probably score with this man. However, if you are not well-dressed, dignified, and have a low income, you probably won't even get to first base with this man. It's really sad that some men just can't accept you as you are.

There's a way around this if you want to do some acting and lying. You can look rich and act rich even though you are not rich. People are judged first by their appearance. All you have got to do is wear the latest expensive-looking fashions for women and be well groomed. Also, you will probably have to do some lying about your wealth. If you think you can play this role to mingle with rich men, give it a try. Some women will try anything, including lying, to attract a man.

The Shy Man

Just like there are many shy women at nightclubs, there are just as many shy men. The shy man is easy to spot. They just stand around all night and don't make an effort to approach women or ask them to dance.

Some are even too shy to dance, so if you ask this man to dance and he says no, it may just be because he's too shy to dance and not because he's rejecting you. In this case, try to strike up a conversation with him. If this fails, move on.

This man will show his shyness in various ways. Below are just a few examples:

1. While talking to you, his eyes will glance off to side or down towards the floor. Shy men have difficulty in looking at a woman in the eyes while talking to her.
2. He may be lacking in conversational skills. He may be rather quiet, speaking in a low voice and not have very much to say. In this case, you will just have to pick up the slack and do most of the talking yourself.
3. If he has a nice physique, he may try to conceal it by wearing clothes that don't compliment his body.
4. Upon meeting him, he will act very nervous. He may tap his fingers on the top of the table or he may tap his feet. He might even bite his nails.
5. While talking, he may stutter quite frequently.
6. When you pay him a compliment, he blushes or does not agree with your compliment.

In conclusion, don't pass up an opportunity to attract or meet a shy man. Once you break the ice and get them warmed up, they can make your night worthwhile.

FINDING MR. RIGHT

The Egotist

Unfortunately, these type of people exist in all phases of life and you will see your share of them in the nightclubs.

This man is a stuck up snob and thinks he's God's gift to women. He walks around the club with his nose up in the air. If you try to stop him and talk to him, he just ignores you and keeps on walking. This is very annoying to you women. It wouldn't hurt him to be friendly and talk to you. Also, out on the dance floor he will be constantly looking at himself in the mirrors, if there happen to be mirrors on the dance floor. He loves looking at himself.

The egotists are difficult to approach because they think they are too good for you. Don't let this discourage you though. At least make an attempt to meet him and if you fail, there are usually plenty of friendly men to meet. Anyway, you would probably take a friendly man over a snob any day.

The Nightclub Regulars

These are the men that you'll see time and time again at the nightclubs. They are what I call "regulars." Their whole life revolves around the nightclubs. You can find them at the clubs two or three times during the week nights and just about every weekend.

Some of these men rarely date. Their whole social life is at the nightclubs with their friends. If he belongs to his own little group of friends, it may be difficult to meet this man. He may just associate and dance with his friends only and consider you an intruder.

If you determine that a man is a regular, don't let this discourage you. He can be met just as easy as any other man. The key to getting in good with this man is becoming a regular yourself. This has numerous advantages because you'll become a familiar face to the other regular men. Just keep going to the nightclubs as much as possible and make it a point to meet and mingle with the men you see there regularly. After going to

Meeting Men in Nightclubs

a particular club regularly, it will be easy to spot the male regulars. When you become a regular yourself, you'll get to know these men on a physical and intimate basis.

The Nightclub Ego-Man

I will describe what I call the "Nightclub EgoMan" that you will run into at nightclubs. This is the guy you will see standing around, depending on his looks to meet women. He may be very handsome or he just thinks he is. He just stands around all night thinking that he's Gods gift to women and he waits for women to approach him. He keeps on waiting and waiting, never making the effort or going out of his way to approach and meet women. I don't need to tell you that this type of man is not very successful at meeting or attracting women.

What to Wear

Now we come to clothes. This can make you or break you and is very important. Clothes do make the woman you know. Nothing will turn off a man more if you are dressed like a slob. Of course, if he's a slob too, he won't care. A decent man admires a woman that is well-groomed and well dressed. Here are some do's and don'ts of nightclub dressing:

1. Don't wear a business suit. This creates a conservative "stuffy" look. Besides you don't want to look like a man. You want to create a feminine look.
2. Whatever you do, don't wear a T-shirt with a slogan on it.
3. Try and wear lightweight material that is cool and not too tight. You're really going to perspire out there on the dance floor and you will feel very uncomfortable if you have got on something hot and heavy.
4. Avoid wearing any clothes with glitter material. This is out!
5. Don't overdress.
6. You can get some fashion ideas by watching dance shows

FINDING MR. RIGHT

such as "Soul Train" and "American Bandstand."
7. While you're in nightclubs, look around at the other women and you can get some fashion ideas from them.
Try to select way-out or unusual unique outfits. These will immediately catch the eye of men. By wearing an unusual and unique outfit and being among people in ordinary clothes, you will find yourself to be the center of attention. This is what you want to do and that is, attract a man's attention.
Try to select sexy-looking clothes. By wearing sexy-looking clothes, you will be sending out a message. The message being that you yourself are also sexually stimulating.
Selection of eye-catching colors are very important in attracting attention. The human eye notices color and form simultaneously. If both your colors and form are unusual, strong, and simple, the human eye must take notice to them. The impression will be strong and quick.
Don't go to extremes though, in your selection of clothes and color. Wearing weird clothes that have too strong and conflicting colors will have the opposite effect in attracting attention. You will repel and you will be labeled as some kind of "weirdo."
One last item on dressing that really turns on and attracts men. When buying clothes, buy them tight-fitting, especially in the buttock and breast area. You will be amazed at the men that will stare at your body. Of course the more endowed you are, the bigger showing you're going to make.
It's a known fact that men are attracted to a nice body. So, why not give them something to drool over, like bulging breasts or a nice ass.

Getting Ready and Psyched Up

Psyching yourself up and making preparations before going to a nightclub are very important. Be sure and get a good nights sleep before you go out. At least seven to eight hours will be sufficient. Eat a good steak dinner with your choice of vegetables prior to going out. This will put a lining on your stomach if you do a lot of heavy drinking and besides that, it will make you feel good.

If you don't have any good dancing records, buy as many as you can afford. There is a reason for this. A couple of hours before you leave, play your favorite records, or if you have a favorite radio station, turn that on. The purpose of this is to get you in the mood for dancing and the nightclub scene.

If you drink, while you are relaxing and listening to the music, drink some of your favorite wine or mixed drinks. Also, taking a hot bath is very relaxing. It's a lot cheaper to drink at home than it is at the clubs. So try to do most of your drinking at home if you want to save some money.

While you are relaxing, picture in your minds eye, meeting some gorgeous hunk at the nightclub. Actually see yourself talking to him, dancing with him, feeling your body rub against his during a slow song, etc.. Feel his body next to yours, feel his crotch grinding against yours. See yourself leaving the nightclub and taking him to your place or going to his place.

You are probably wondering what's the purpose of creating all these images in your mind. These images will register in your subconscious mind and when you get to the nightclub your subconscious mind will give directions to your conscious mind to act them out. Don't be disappointed if this does not work the first time because it takes repetition for this to soak into your subconscious mind. Also, all day long on the day you're going out, keep telling yourself over and over, "I'm going to meet a man tonight." You will be amazed at the results. This will also help you develop a positive mental attitude and build up your self-confidence.

About thirty minutes before you leave, practice dancing in front of the mirror and looking as sexy as you can. Develop that "I want to make love to you look" in your eyes. Also, practice smiling in front of the mirror. I'm talking about a nice warm friendly smile, not a phony smile showing all of your teeth.

If you have a cute and sexy smile, use it on men. If you don't have a nice smile, you had better invent one. A good smile can literally melt a man. This makes them feel really special and appreciated. So, practice that sexy smile of yours because it's going to do wonders for you when you approach or when you are approached by men in nightclubs. Before you know it you will be meeting men with just your sexy smile alone.

When approaching a man, always turn on that smile of yours. If you approach him with a real serious and nervous look on your face, you just might frighten him. Just a warm, friendly, and relaxed smile will do wonders when it comes to meeting men at nightclubs.

Drugs

I do not advocate the use of drugs and I'm not writing this to promote the use of drugs. I'm merely going to expose some of the nightclub drug scene and how some women use drugs to pick up and meet men.

It is a known fact that before going to a nightclub some men and women take drugs to get high. Why? Some use drugs to calm them down so they will not feel so uptight. Others use them to help them get into the music and lights. Of course, there are those that are just hooked on drugs.

I will expose some of the ways women use drugs to meet and pick up men. Before leaving for the nightclub she will roll a couple of joints and carry them with her or leave them in the car. After meeting a man in the club, she will ask him if he would like to go smoke a joint. Then they will either go to her place or go for a ride in the car to smoke a joint.

I have female friends who have occasionally been asked if they have a joint. Although none of them smoked, if they did this would present a golden opportunity them to get acquainted. Women also use uppers, downers, and cocaine to get men to leave the nightclubs with them. Drugs will make a man lose his inhibitions and make some men very horny, depending on which drugs he has taken.

In conclusion, I do not recommend the use of drugs for meeting men because drugs are illegal, even though some may be harmless. Still the nightclub drug scene will go on and on.

It's really sad that some people have to take drugs before

Meeting Men in Nightclubs

going to clubs to feel good and have a good time. You can have just as good of time doing a little social drinking. At least it's legal.

Nightclub "Hot Spots"

As a general rule, it is best to arrive early at a nightclub so you can check out the action. If you arrive late, sometimes most of the men will be taken up. Of course there are some nightclubs that do not get going until after midnight. Most men start coming in from 9-11 PM, as a general rule. The men who are shift workers start coming in after 11PM. Ideally, the best time to arrive is around 9PM. This way you can see what comes thru the door and size up your prospects for the night.

Don't worry about getting a table in the beginning because you are going to be on your feet making the rounds. However, if there is a male prospect sitting at the bar, by all means go and sit beside him and strike up a conversation.

When the action starts picking up, there's going to be favorable places to be standing while approaching the men.

Some women like to stand around by the door and approach a man as he comes in. This does not work too well because of the following reasons:

1. When they first walk in they want to go to the restroom. Afterall, when nature calls you tend to be in a hurry and don't care to stop and talk to a stranger.

2. They want to go to the restroom to make sure that they look attractive.

3. They want to go to the restroom to take drugs.

4. They want to cruise around the nightclub to see if any of their friends are there.

5. They want to walk around to check out the available women.

6. They want to go straight to the bar first to buy a drink.

So you see, it's really not a good idea to stand around and approach them as they walk in. You can go ahead and try it but you will have a lot more success in other areas of the club

25

which I am about to describe.

One of the best places to stand is by the dance floor, especially if you dance. It's even better if the path to the mens restroom goes right by the dance floor. There are men who purposely stand around the dance floor to ask women to dance or to get asked to dance themselves. This makes it quite easy to ask them to dance or to get asked to dance by hanging around this area. This is such a great area for making "contact." Also, some men like to get a table around the dance floor so they are more likely to get asked to dance.

Another area that is excellent is around the entrance to the mens restroom. Every man will go the restroom at least once and many times if he's drinking a lot. It's usually not a good idea to approach them before they go into the restroom because they are usually in a hurry to relieve themselves. There is a way around this though, by simply saying, "Can I talk to you when you come out of the restroom?" Normally it is better to approach them when they are coming out of the restroom.

Flirting

While you are cruising the nightclub, keep your flirting eyes out for the man that is alone. He is usually the easiest to meet and attract. He is there for a reason and you can be the lucky woman to fulfill that reason.

Also while walking, keep that sexy-looking gleam in your eye. Literally try to melt men with your eyes. If you make eye contact with a man make sure you give him a friendly smile and if he is close enough to you, simply say, "Hi." That is all it takes and with practice it will come easy.

If you make eye contact with some man across the way from you and he turns away, don't give up on him. Try to make eye contact again and smile at him. If he smiles back, approach him immediately! This is an opportunity that must not be passed up because it's an open invitation for you to come over and introduce yourself or ask him to dance.

Whatever you do, don't stare at a man. This is impolite and

Meeting Men in Nightclubs

nobody likes to be stared at. Just look at him long enough to make it quite clear that you see him and then immediately look away. What you are saying with your eyes when you look at him this way is, "I know you are there and I would not dream of invading your privacy. Just keep looking at him off and on until you establish some meaningful eye contact and exchange smiles. So, there you have it, the art of flirting.

What really amazes me is these women at the nightclubs that don't even flirt with men. They just stare into space or look down at the floor. If they do accidently catch the eye of a man, they look away as quickly as possible and let it go at that. They just don't know what they are missing and what they are missing out on is meeting men the easy way.

So my friend, if you're like this, make it a point to stop staring into space and start flirting with men. Flirt with every man in sight. It's a lot of fun and you will be attracting more men than ever before.

How to Approach a Man

Quite simply, all it takes to meet a man in a nightclub is to just walk up to him and start talking to him or by asking him to dance. There's a lot of women who just stand around all night too scared to approach a man or they think they will be approached themselves. Believe me, I know from experience that sometimes you won't meet a lot of men just standing around waiting for them to make the first move. It helps to make the first move and it comes quite easy after you practice at it. Enough about shy women at clubs. I'm devoting two chapters on shyness and how to overcome this problem.

You're probably wondering "What do I say when I approach a man?" Here are just a few simple opening lines which work well. Feel free to make up your own.
1. "Hi! My name is_____."
2. "Why are you flirting with me?"
3. "What's your name?"
4. "Are you having a good time?"

FINDING MR. RIGHT

5. "What's that cologne you're wearing?"
6. "I love your hair. Where do you have it done?"
7. "Would you like to dance?"
8. "Are you a model?" (Quite a compliment to men)
9. "What kind of drink is that?"
10. This one really works well. Try it and see for yourself. "Excuse me for being so forward, but I could not help but admire the way you danced. Where did you learn to dance like that?" This lays the foundation for starting a conversation. Then you can ask him, "What do you do for a living?", and so on. Then you can ask him to dance.

Many women feel very uncomfortable when approaching men. You're going to have to resolve here and now to put away all your shy ways, fear of rejection, and the other restrictive barriers that keep you from meeting men that you are attracted to. You must assume responsibility for making social contact with men. No matter what technique you use to approach men and no matter how often you use these techniques, you're going to feel a certain amount of discomfort. This is only natural. You must bear the responsibility for meeting others, despite this discomfort.

If you have difficulty approaching men, try this exercise. Force yourself to meet and approach ten men each time you go a nightclub. Your goal doesn't have to be ten men. You can make it any number you desire. Make it a realistic number though. The main thing is setting that goal. This gives you something to work for and something to accomplish. Look upon this exercise as just practice. Practice for building your social skills for meeting men. Gradually your difficulty in approaching men will disappear. Try this exercise. It really works!

One point you must remember. Most men like to be approached at nightclubs. That's what they are there for. To meet a girl like yourself.

In conclusion, you must not forget to approach the bartenders also. They are usually attractive and friendly. Some may not even have girlfriends due to the unusual hours that

Meeting Men in Nightclubs

they work. Always make it a point to talk to them and get to know them on a first name basis. They don't have much time to talk on the job, but after they start seeing you and talking to you and waiting on you, you'll establish a friendly rapport. Then just ask them out on their day off. You've got nothing to lose!

Fast-Dancing

If you don't dance, you'd better learn because a lot of men go to nightclubs to dance and have a good time. You don't have to invest a lot of money in private dancing lessons either. Many cities offer inexpensive dance classes with groups, or perhaps you have a female friend who will teach you.

You don't have to learn fancy dance steps. Just basic free-style dance steps will be sufficient. Besides, in a lot of nightclubs the dance floor is so crowded, there's just not enough room to do any of the sophisticated dance steps, especially on the weekend.

When approaching a man to ask him to dance, whatever you do don't fondle him, paw at his body, or put your arm around his shoulders or waist. This turns some men off when a stranger starts pawing at his body. This approach is just too fast for most men and it scares them. Just simply walk up next to him and say with a smile, "Would you like to dance?" If he says, "No" just say "OK." You might also say, "Thanks anyway" or even better, "How about later?" Don't stand there and aggravate him by arguing with him as to why he won't dance with you. Just go on to the next guy and so on until you find someone to dance with.

Also, look for a man tapping his feet or moving his body to the beat of the music. This usually means that he is anxious to dance. If he's dancing with himself while standing, this also means that he's dying to dance.

Don't forget to dance to the slow songs, even though they don't play too many at most nightclubs. Don't pass up these good opportunities to get instant physical contact with men.

FINDING MR. RIGHT

So now you're out on the dance floor dancing to a fast song. While you're dancing with him, make eye contact. Just catch his eye and hold it momentarily, then look away. Repeat this process until you start getting a smile out of him or at least a look of interest. Of course, now some men won't look at you while you are dancing. They don't focus their eyes on anyone in particular and look at their feet, the floor, or they're busy trying to show off in front of everyone else. Some men are self-conscious about everybody watching them, so they don't make much eye contact. Anyway, try to establish as much eye contact as possible. This will be to your advantage.

While you're dancing this first dance together, be sure and make some verbal contact no matter how loud the music is. The first thing you should say is, "What's your name?" After he tells you his name, tell him yours. Now you have become formally introduced, just by dancing. Also, make a comment on how nice he looks or compliment his clothes, jewelry, smile, etc.

So now this first song is coming to an end. When it ends don't hesitate and look at him to see if he wants to dance to the next record. Just turn away from him while continuing to dance and look at him out of the corner of your eye to see what he is going to do. You see, by hesitating at the end of a song, you force a direct confrontation on whether to dance to the next song. If you just keep on dancing into the next song, taking it for granted that he wants to dance again, you'll be more successful in keeping him out on the dance floor. The longer you dance with him the better your chances of getting to know him.

Now we get to the part when you finish dancing. This will usually end in these following ways:

1. He stops dancing and says, "Thank you."
2. You're both hot, sweaty, and exhausted from dancing and mutually agree to leave the dance floor.
3. Either one of you develops a cramp and has to leave the dance floor. Has this ever happen to you?

This is very important! After you have finished dancing whatever you do, don't let him get away after thanking you for the dance. Just simply say, "Can I join you for a drink?" Also,

Meeting Men in Nightclubs

you could say, "Can I talk to you about something?" After this statement, he will say, "Talk about what?" Then you say, "I'll tell you when you when we sit down." After this, just start making conversation. Also, if he doesn't have a table and he is just standing like yourself, just say, "Can I talk to you for a little while?"

So, what you do after you finish dancing can determine the future of your whole night and whether you're going to become intimate with a man or not. What I can't figure out is these women that dance with a man and don't even look at or talk to him while they are dancing and when they finish, she says, "Thanks" and just walks away. Needless to say, you don't meet any men this way.

So when you have finished dancing, move right in for the kill. Don't hesitate, just proceed immediately with determination that you're going to make contact with this man.

Slow-Dancing

Let me give you a few pointers if you're slow-dancing and by all means try to dance to every slow dance because of the physical contact involved.

Just as in fast dancing, immediately start introduction procedures. Open up by saying, "My name is_____ What's yours?

When slow-dancing, try to hold him as close to your body as possible. Gently now! Don't squeeze him like an octopus. When moving your right leg, gently brush his inner thighs. While dancing, gently squeeze his hand and see if you get any response. If you do, continue with the next step. Start rubbing his back with your hand. At this point if he starts rubbing your shoulders, neck, or back and starts grinding his crotch against yours, you are on your way. At this stage of the game it's time to try and kiss him. Begin kissing his neck and work your way up to behind the ear, then the ear lobe, then kiss him on the lips. If you've gotten this far, chances are you're going to become intimate with him tonight, if not later for sure.

FINDING MR. RIGHT

If you have tried all these moves and you do not get any response, don't be concerned about it. Some men are reluctant to show any affection towards a total stranger. This is quite common, so don't jump to conclusions thinking that he's cold or not interested in you.

Whatever you do, don't give up on a man who does not respond to your physical advances while slow-dancing. Just follow up with your conversational skills and get to know him better and get him to like you. Perhaps then he will loosen up when he gets to know you a little bit better and becomes interested in you. If you use good pick-up techniques, you shouldn't have any problems.

In conclusion, here's a profile of the typical man you will meet in nightclubs: The typical average man in a nightclub is a blue-collar worker. His income is middle to lower class (he earns between fifteen thousand and thirty thousand dollars annually-1988 figures).

Most likely he has not attended college and is a high school graduate. He is usually under thirty-five years of age (the average age range of men who go to nightclubs is between twenty-five and thirty-four). He most likely has been divorced a couple of times and has been single for more than three years.

According to one intensive and reliable survey conducted, only one out of every ten men at nightclubs is a financially successful bachelor. So, if you're looking for a rich man, this is not the place to go. There is one exception and that is the exclusive "membership only" nightclubs.

EXCLUSIVE INTERVIEWS WITH SINGLE MEN

What Kind of Woman Turns You Off?

Steve L. - "Tall, skinny women. Fat women really turn me off."
Jerry W. - "Ugly women, body defects, lacking conversational skills, conceited."
William D. - "Women who do nothing but gripe and complain about anything and everything."
Syed R. - "Unattractive (face and body), unintelligent and ill-mannered, also one who does not have good taste for dressing and not matching in age group."
Bob W. - "Golddiggers. Women who are just interested in how much money you have, what kind of car you drive, what you do for a living, etc. I want to be liked for myself, not my material wealth."
Lee B. - "Women who come on too strong and demand too much commitment before I'm even ready for a commitment."
Bill V. - "Women you can't carry on a conversation with. Their answers to questions are just "yes" and "no" and they don't offer any comments or ideas of their own."
Brent F. - "A silly woman who does nothing but laugh all the time really gets on my nerves."
Paul G. - "Career women. Their whole life revolves around their work. Some don't have much time for dating and don't want to be tied down to a relationship."
Don D. - "Cold, unresponsive women. One who talks excessively and not a good listener. Obese women and I dislike real short hair on women."

What Kind of Woman Turns You On?

Steve L. - "I prefer a woman with a medium build and long hair. Also, I like a good conversationalist."
Jerry W. - "Good-looking with a symmetrical body. Young women turn me on."
William D. - "A woman who shows interest in me, physically appealing, and makes me feel comfortable."
Syed R. - "Beautiful, attractive appearance, age 24-32, good figure, average intelligence, appealingly dressed, romantic and informally seductive."
Bob W. - "A woman with a body and face right out of Playboy Magazine."
Lee B. - "A woman who can have multiple orgasms and sexually experienced. Also, a woman who gives a good massage."
Bill V. - "A woman who moans and groans with sounds of appreciation and pleasure when we make love."
Brent F. - "A woman with a good personality and a good sense of humor. A girl who makes me laugh."
Paul G. - "Women who talk about sex."
Don D. - "A woman who's like one on the guys. She likes the outdoors, sports, likes to drink, etc.. Sexy women who wear tight-fitting clothes. An affectionate and romantic woman."

What is Your Biggest Obstacle to Picking Up a Woman?

Steve L. - "When I'm sober. I need to have a couple of drinks, so I can build up my nerve to approach women."
Jerry W. - "I think most women are too respectable to be picked up."
William D. - "Women who seem to be frightened when you try to approach them."
Syed R. - "Time is the biggest factor. I do not like going to bars to pick up women."
Bob W. - "Sometimes I just can't get up the nerve to approach a woman."
Lee B. - "I guess you could sum it up as fear. Fear that I'm going to fail when I try to pick her up."
Bill V. - "Some women look stuck-up and conceited, therefore they seem unapproachable."
Brent F. - "I have this fear of being rejected. I just haven't learned how to handle rejection yet."
Paul G. - "I don't have any obstacles. Picking up women is easy for me."
Don D. - "Sometimes I get depressed at nightclubs and just stand around all night and don't try to meet any women."

Do You Feel It's OK For a Woman to Ask a Man Out For a Date?

Steve L. - "No, I guess I'm old fashioned. I think the man should do the asking and I'd be offended if a woman ask me out."

Jerry W. - "Of course. If she feels that she wanted a particular man badly, she must ask him for a date."

William D. - "I'm not one to turn down a date if I like a woman and if she makes the first move, that's OK with me."

Syed R. - "Yes, I like to be pursued by women. They can chase me all they want!"

Bob W. - "Not for the first date. I don't mind thereafter."

Lee B. - "Not particularly. I enjoy the chase and this kind of takes the fun out of it."

Bill V. - "This is fine with me but I interpret it as a sexual come-on."

Brent F. - "Yes, but I've never been asked out for a date by a woman."

Paul G. - "Yes, and I'm so glad times have changed. It's now acceptable for a woman to ask a man out."

Don D. - "That's fine with me. If I'm attracted to her, I'll definitely accept. I really admire a woman with courage and guts."

What is The Most Frequent Reason You Stop Dating a Particular Woman?

Steve L. - "When a woman starts getting possessive and jealous. This scares me away."
Jerry W. - "If she is not ready to go to bed after I spend a couple hundred bucks on her."
William D. - "She doesn't show interest in me anymore."
Syed R. - "Afraid I'll end up getting married, if we get too serious."
Bob W. - "With my nature, I go out with a woman a few times and then it's time for me to move on."
Lee B. - "I find her boring and dull. Also, very superficial."
Bill V. - "She puts too much pressure on me in the beginning to become intimately involved with her."
Brent F. - "A woman who has emotional problems, is immature, or neurotic."
Paul G. - "A woman who refuses to have sex with me. There's nothing I hate worse than being sexually frustrated."
Don D. - "Lack of chemistry and communication. Also, I don't like to string a woman along if the relationship is just not working."

How Do You Feel About Women Who Initiate Sex?

Steve L. - "I have no objections to a woman initiating sex. This would be a big turn on."

Jerry W. - "I like this. If she wants me, I will satisfy her."

William D. - "For some reason, I attract women like this and it's really nice when a man doesn't have to work hard to initiate sex."

Syed R. - "At a desirable place and situation, it's acceptable. In privacy, definitely enjoyable."

Bob W. - "In some respects, it's degrading to a woman. It makes me think the woman is promiscuous and has loose morals."

Lee B. - "This is a real relief to me and takes the pressure off me because generally, it's left up to me to initiate sex with most women I date."

Bill V. - "As a general rule, I don't care if a woman takes the lead and aggressive role, but sometimes I'm curious if there isn't an ulterior motive behind it."

Brent F. - "I don't mind if the woman takes the lead, but I don't particularly care to be undressed or lead into the bedroom. I like a woman who undresses me with her eyes."

Paul G. - "It's OK if it's done in a soft way, with a feminine touch. If done in an aggressive manner, it turns me off."

Don D. - "Love it! There's nothing I enjoy more than being seduced by a woman. This is a super turn on!"

CHAPTER TWO

Where to Meet Men

The following recommendations on where to meet men is the most extensive information on this subject ever published:

The Hitchhiker

How many times have you seen a guy thumbing for a ride? At least once and probably many times.

Like most women, you probably just passed these men and kept right on going. Well girl, you just passed up a potential golden opportunity.

I know what you're thinking already. It's too dangerous to pick up men thumbing for a ride. The majority of hitchhikers are not dangerous. I'll leave it up to you if you want to take advantage of this opportunity to meet men.

So the next time you see a male hitchhiker, consider picking him up. If he's going the opposite direction, make a U-turn and go back and pick him up.

You are probably wondering now what to do after you have

FINDING MR. RIGHT

picked him up. The first thing to do is ask him where he's going. This will give you an idea of how far he intends to ride with you and you'll know how much time you'll have to make your approach.

If you'll follow my conversational guidelines outlined in my chapter on how to talk to a man, you'll establish a warm rapport. After you've established some friendly contact, just ask him, "Why don't we drive over to my place and have a drink? If he declines, tell him, "I'd like to see you again. Would you mind if I give you a call sometime?" Hopefully he will give you his phone number and you can follow up on him later.

If you're traveling out of town and pick up a man on the highway, ask him if he'd like to stop and get a motel room to get cleaned up and relax.

Parties

Never, never turn down a party invitation. Whether it be a friends, a beach party, office party, etc. Parties are a real gold mine for meeting men. The atmosphere is very sociable and conducive for flirtations.

All you've got to do is walk up to a man you're interested in and introduce yourself. Then follow up with your conversational skills.

Also, it's a good idea to throw your own party. Invite everyone you can think of. For instance, if it's a female friend you invite, ask her to invite some of her male friends. If it's a male friend, ask him to invite some of his male friends. This way your party will be stocked with an ample supply of men. This will give you an opportunity to meet some new men and make friends.

When at a party, whatever you do, don't stand in a corner. Be sure to mingle and flirt with as many men as possible. There's nothing to fear because people will be friendly and rejections are rare unless you make a fool of yourself.

Where to Meet Men

Daytime Barflys

These are men who hang out at bars during the day. They are bored and horny and looking for some action. There's a place in Houston called The Four Palms and this place is crawling with men during the day. Most of them are there for one reason and that's to meet women.

So if you're off during the day, check out your local bars during the day. If you see a man alone in the bar, approach him immediately and ask him, "Can I join you for some conversation?"

Volunteer Activities

There are numerous organizations looking for voluntary workers. By doing volunteer work, you will most likely be exposed to some nice men and you will be working together for a common cause. You just can't help but get to know men well when you're working together. This leaves the door wide open for forming intimate relationships.

There are plenty of activities that you can volunteer for. Examples are: Charity work, political campaigns, hospital work, crisis hot-line counselors, church functions, working with retarded and underprivileged children, telethons, carnivals, bazaars, teaching courses, party host, and many, many more.

How do you find volunteer work? Just check your newspapers. Here in Houston there's a special section in the newspaper listing organizations looking for volunteers, giving details and how to contact them. Keep your eyes and ears open for volunteer opportunities.

Volunteer for anything. Even if it's your job. Volunteer for special functions such as company picnics, dinners, banquets, planning company trips, recreation committee, etc. This will pay off in contacts with all those eligible men at work.

FINDING MR. RIGHT

Hotels and Motels

I realize it could be expensive to just rent a room for a day, in hope of meeting men. However, it could pay off in big dividends. What you can do to cut down on expenses is to share the room with a couple of girlfriends and all three of you go man-hunting.

Hotels and motels are great places to approach the world's easiest target for casual sex (the man on business trip or vacation). He's more relaxed and casual and he's away from the prying eyes of family, friends, and neighbors. He will let his hair down and he doesn't have to worry about his reputation or what people think, being that he's away from home.

The best places to approach men are at the pool, club, or restaurant.

In conclusion, I might add that if you don't want to rent a room, you can still meet men at hotels and motels. The clubs are open to the public, so it's free game in there and it's a good place to hang out and meet out-of-towners. Also, you can drive to a hotel or motel in your bathing suit and hang around the pool and strike up a conversation with all those men. Be sure and bring a change of clothes with you in case you want to go somewhere afterwards.

Parks

This is a great place to meet men. Some men go by themselves to meditate and think about their problems. Some go to read and even some go just to meet girls.

If you see a man all alone looking sad and blue, approach him and say, "You look sad, can I be of any help?" He just may pour his heart out to you.

If you see a man walking a dog, approach him and say, "That sure is a cute dog you have there. What's his name?" This can open the door for more conversation.

You might want to bring a frisbee with you and ask a man, "Do you want to toss some frisbee?"

Where to Meet Men

What you can do when you go to a park is bring a picnic blanket, a bottle of wine, and lunch for two. When you spot a man you like, set up your blanket and picnic supplies near him. Then invite him to join you. You can have some fun times this way.

The Supermarket

This is an overlooked place to meet men. These places are just crawling with men. With a little confidence, this is an excellent place to approach men.

Here's some examples of approaches to use: Hang around the meat section and when you see a man you'd like to meet, approach him and ask him, "How long do you broil chicken?" Then you can follow up with, "Gee, I wish I knew how to cook. How did you learn to cook? Did your mother teach you?" The main objective is to get a conversation going and see if he'd like to get together sometime. Another good place for the approach is in the produce department. Just pick out the vegetable of your choice and ask him how to cook it.

Tennis

Take a look around at the tennis courts. What will you see? Plenty of men. That's what. Tennis is very popular and attracts a lot of men. Lots of men go to the tennis courts to meet women. Perhaps not openly, but subconsciously.

Tennis is a one-on-one sport and this allows for a lot of mental concentration between you. It sure is a good way of getting to know someone. Just the two of you having fun together. What's good too is that after you have played a match, it's quite natural to cool off and talk to each other and perhaps go and have a drink or get a bite to eat.

How do you approach men at the tennis courts? There's a lot of different approaches. You can say, "Do you need a partner?" Or you could reserve a court in advance and say to a man, "Would you like to play on Court 9? My tennis partner

FINDING MR. RIGHT

didn't show up."

You might want to arrive early to shoot the bull before you play tennis. Just talk to any and every man you see. This way you can meet men before you even make it to the courts.

If you don't play tennis, by all means take lessons. This opens up another avenue for meeting men. Let me say that you don't have to become an expert. Basic skills will get you by.

I would suggest playing at public tennis courts. You'll see more of a variety of different men there. Tennis clubs are very expensive and you'll see the same old faces a lot.

A word about tennis attire. It would be worth it to invest in some nice pro-type tennis wear. It will make you look like a tennis pro and these outfits really turn some men on.

In conclusion, I want to tell you about a device to use to attract men and makes you popular. When you play tennis just always bring a large jug filled with lemonaide, kool-aid, or Gator-Aide. Also, you can even I bring a small ice chest filled with cokes. All you have to do is ask a man on the court, "Would you like something cold to drink?" After you've worked up a sweat or if it's a hot day, something cold to drink really hits the spot and is hard to turn down.

Rafting Trips

Want a thrill of a lifetime and meet men at the same time? I'm a whitewater enthusiast and the excitement of shooting the rapids is indescribable. It is truly an experience that you will carry to your grave.

I'd recommend taking the overnight excursions. These can range from two to fourteen days. However, there are one day and half-day trips available. You could even take the one day trip three or four different days and meet even more men.

What's really ideal about these trips, are that when you start out everyone are complete strangers, but this doesn't last long because you'll get to know each other fast. You'll be camping, rafting, cooking and eating together, and sleeping with a dozen or more people. In this group there will be some single

Where to Meet men

men. These shared conditions are ideal for a romance to begin.
Because of the closeness involved, you'll make female friends also. These friendships can extend long after the trip is over.

Where do I find out about rafting trips? You can contact any travel agency or some of them are advertised in newspapers.

Being that I'm a rafting enthusiast, I have a lot of sources that you can contact for information on their rafting trips. They are as follows:

Worldwide River Tours, Inc.
37 Chaparral
New Braunfels, TX 78130
Toll-free 1-800-531-7927 in U.S., 1-800-292-7879 (Texas)

Trips range from 1 to 29 days. Trips available in U.S.: Oregon, California, Idaho, Utah, Texas, West Virginia, Arizona, Alaska, and Colorado. Trips are available worldwide: Ethiopia, India, Turkey, Tanzania, Nepal, Peru, Chile, New Guinea, Pakistan, Yugoslavia, Australia, New Zealand, Canada, Guatemala, and Mexico. Call for prices.

Texas Canoe Trails, Inc.
Star Rt.3 Box 866B
New Braunfels, TX 78130
Phone: (512) 355-2212

Trips range from 2 to 17 days. Prices range from $110 to $600 per person (check current prices). Trips available in Texas, Colorado, and Mexico. Call and ask about any additional trips.

Fort Lee Co.
Box 2103
Marble Canyon, AZ 86036
Phone: (602) 355-2212

One day and eight day trips available. One day trip cost $29.95 per person and the 8 day trip is $595 per person (check current prices). The one day trip is 15 miles down the Colorado

45

FINDING MR. RIGHT

River near Page, Arizona. The eight day trip goes thru the Grand Canyon (killer rapids!).

Colorado Adventures, Inc.
Box 851
Steamboat Springs, CO 80477
Toll free in Colorado 1-800-332-3200
    One to three day trips available down a variety of exciting rivers in Colorado: The Colorado River, Arkansas, North Platte, and the Upper Elk. One day trip prices range from $27 to $35 (check current prices).

Whitewater Voyagers
Box 346
Poncha Springs, CO 81242
Phone: (303) 539-4821 7:30 AM - 6:00 PM
        (303) 539-2776 after hours
    One half to three day trips available. Trips are down the Arkansas River. Prices range from $15 to $125 per person (check current prices).

Texas River Expeditions
Reservations and Information call (713) 497-8696 or 497-8696
    Two to six day trips available. Prices range from $65 to $600 per person. Trips available in Texas, New Mexico, Arkansas, and Idaho.

Parkland Expeditions, Inc.
Box 371
Jackson, WY 83001
Phone: (307) 733-3379
    They offer a five day raft trip thru Grand Teton National Park down the Snake River. This is what I consider the most beautiful national park in the U.S. and I've been to most of the major ones. The view is absolutely breath-taking. Write or call for further information.

Where to Meet Men

Jogging

Jogging is a fantastic way to meet men and besides that, it's good for your health, mind and body.

Pick out a jogging area and start running on a regular basis. By observation, you will notice men that arrive each day at the same place and around the same time. Jogging trails and parks are wonderful for unhurried seduction, because you're going to see him again and again, so you can work on him a little at a time.

During the week the men are usually out between 6 and 8 AM, around noon, and between 5 and 8 PM. Weekends are usually best because you will see them jogging throughout the day.

Let me explain the approach to use on jogging trails that will work well for you. Always jog with a towel around your neck and wear a small plastic bottle filled with lemonaide, Gator-Aid, or water around your neck. Then you will jog beside a man and offer him a drink and your towel to wipe the sweat off of his face. Then you invite him to sit down and take a breather so you can talk.

Roller Rinks

This is a hot new activity that has swept the nation. The roller discos are particularly popular. They have light shows and a good sound system.

It may have never occurred to you that this is a hot spot for meeting men. Believe me, these places are abundant with men. A lot of them go to the rinks to meet women.

You might be saying to yourself, "I'd like to go but I don't know how to skate." Well don't let that hold you back. Skating is very easy and you'll be able to pick it up rather quickly without lessons. Of course, with practice, you'll get a lot better. If you don't have skates, that's no problem. You can rent them.

If you're a good skater and you see a man having problems, offer to help him learn how to skate. He will appreciate it and

FINDING MR. RIGHT

this is another good way to meet men at the rink.

Art Galleries

Go to any art gallery (especially on the weekends) and you'll see some men. Some of these men aren't just there because of their appreciation for art. They are there to meet a girl like yourself.

An art gallery provides a perfect setting to approach men. The atmosphere is very friendly and the men aren't going to feel uptight and threatened when you try to meet them.

Approaching a man in an art gallery is very simple. All you have to do is walk over to a man standing in front of a painting and make a comment on the painting. Another variation to this is to stand in front of a painting yourself and when a man passes by, you make a comment to him about the painting. After you've made contact say, "Would you mind if I tour the gallery with you?" Afterwards you can invite him out to get something to eat or to go have a drink somewhere.

Skiing

Skiing resorts are real "hot" meeting spots consisting of mostly singles and groups. You won't see many couples and you will see plenty of men. I'd highly recommend spending part of your annual vacation at a ski resort.

How do I plan a skiing vacation? Just contact your local travel agent and they will be able to assist you. Some airlines offer ski tour packages and charter flights. These charter flights are golden opportunities because all of you will be going to the same destination. You'll be able to make friends on the plane. Be sure and sit next to a man or a group of men. Then just strike up a conversation. This way you can have some men lined up before you even get to the resort.

You may be saying to yourself, "I don't know how to ski." Well this is no problem. There will be a lot of beginners there just like yourself. You'll need to take lessons and there's a lot

Where to Meet Men

of advantages to this. You'll be exposed to lots of men in the class and will have opportunities to meet them. Just be sure and take group lessons so you'll be exposed to a number of men.

You can meet men first at the ski lift. Everyone will be standing around chatting while waiting to go up the lift. Being that most lifts have chairs built for two, just ask a man, "Would you like to ride up with me?" Most rides are of a long duration, so you'll have plenty of time to converse on the way up.

Nightlife is booming and the action is hot around the resorts. The bars, nightclubs, and restaurants are loaded with nice men looking for a good time. That's where you come in at.

So what are you waiting for? Why not plan a ski trip and have the time of your life?

Department Stores

These are great places for meeting men and salesmen and are literally just crawling with lots of young attractive men.

Meeting salesmen is very easy. They are usually fairly attractive and are usually bored and would welcome a girl like yourself approaching them and brightening up their day. All you have to do is simply pretend you are shopping for a gift for your father or brother and ask him for assistance. After you have spent some time with him talking and making contact, ask him out to dinner on his lunch break or after he gets off.

As for the shoppers in the stores, let me offer some approaches:

When you see a man loaded down with purchases, offer to help him carry his packages. This has drawbacks though because he might not trust a stranger carrying his packages. He may fear that you'll run off with them. It's worth a try though. All he can do is say no and think of the possibilities if he says yes.

Another approach is to walk up to a man pretending you need help with a purchase. For example, if you're in a jewelry store, approach a man and say, "I'm shopping for a watch for my brother and I was wondering if you would try this

FINDING MR. RIGHT

watch on so I can see how it looks?" 99 out of 100 times he will help you. After that just turn on your charm and conversational skills and ask him out.

A good place to approach men is at the cologne counters. Your approach? Look for a man trying on some cologne and get next to him and give him your opinion of that exotic scent he just tried on.

Restaurants

This is an overlooked place to meet men. Using special techniques, you can be successful in meeting men here. Here are the techniques:

1. If you see a man across the way you'd like to meet, just simply use the waiter or waitress as a messenger. Now, instruct him to bring this man a drink and a note saying, "Hi! My name is Sheena from across the way in the red dress and curly hair and I'm irresistibly attracted to you and I'd love to meet you. Will you come over and join me?"

2. If you see a man you'd like to meet at a counter or table with an empty chair, just make it a point to sit next to him. Then you ask him, "Excuse me, I've never eaten here before and I was wondering if you could recommend something good to eat?" This breaks the ice and then you follow up with your conversational skills.

3. As a variation to technique number one, ask your waiter or waitress to ask the man if he'd mind if the woman in the red dress and curly hair across the way joined him.

Transportation

If you commute by train, bus, plane, subways, etc., there's going to be golden opportunities to meet men. These places are filled with eligible, attractive men.

The whole trick to meeting them is to make it a point to take a seat next to them. This way you've got him pinned in and he's not going anywhere unless you scare him off. If you're on a

Where to Meet Men

train or plane, he doesn't have much choice.

All you've got to do when sitting next to him is to just start talking to him. Talk to him about anything and turn on that charm of yours.

If you take a bus or train to work or school, pick out any male riders you'd like to meet. Select one and make it a point to sit near or close to him. Do this each time you see him and after seeing you a few times you'll practically be old friends, even if you haven't spoken to each other.

Churches

You'll always find plenty of single, nice men at church.

Many churches have begun to sponsor activities for singles. These activities range from dances and trips to lectures and discussions, from seminars on communication to workshops on sexuality.

If the church doesn't have a singles group, you'll have to use the conventional approach. Pick out a church and start going there regularly. Each time you go make it a point to sit next to or near the man of your choice. Try to be near this man each time you go to church. You'll become old friends before too long. The first chance you get, ask him if you could talk to him after the service. He will probably say yes and you'll be on your way.

Human Potential Groups

These groups function to lay the ground work to help people lead a happier and fulfilled life. Examples of such groups are Silva Mind Control, Actualizations, EST, Transactional Analysis, Dale Carnegie courses, etc. A majority of these groups follow the pioneering work of Abraham Maslow and Carl Rogers in humanistic psychology, the therapy groups of the 1960's, and the eclectic Esalen Institute total experience.

These groups provide an excellent vehicle for one to meet

other singles. A large number of people attending these training sessions are unmarried.

Human potential group workshops provide a relaxed atmosphere to meet others. You don't feel pressured to meet others like you would if you were in a singles bar. You're both there for a common cause and this brings people together. The people there are eager to meet others and the men are friendly. These groups create conditions under which friendships and relationships can flourish.

So, why not look into joining one of these groups? It can bring beneficial change into your life and give you new insights, not to mention meeting lots of new men and establishing new friendships.

Health Clubs

This is the best of both worlds. You can get your body into shape while at the same time, shape up your love-life.

They offer activities such as racquetball, swimming, tennis, whirlpools, saunas, and exercise. These offer excellent opportunities for meeting men. All you have to do is ask him to join you in a game of racquetball or even challenge him to a race across the pool. The saunas and whirlpools are hot spots too. Just imagine yourself relaxing in a whirlpool filled with handsome men. Think of the possibilities!

Another advantage which you'll like is, being that the men scantily dressed in their exercise suits or bathing suits, you can get an unobstructed idea of what they'd look like with those few impediments off.

A final word in selecting a health club. Be sure and shop around and check out their facilities. A majority of clubs will give you a free trial day. This way you can check out the men in these clubs and what kind of set up there is for meeting them.

In conclusion, I'd like to mention, you'd be surprised how many men join these clubs just to meet women. Keep this in mind when you become a member, even though it is going to be a little expensive. Believe me, you'll get your moneys worth!

Where to Meet Men

Swimming Pools

This is one of the greatest places to meet men. I'm going to be talking mainly about apartment swimming pools.

Here's the techniques to use successfully to meet men at the pool:

You're going to need some very important equipment. Your appearance is very important and you want to make a good impression upon entering the pool area. I would suggest wearing a revealing bathing suit. Cosmo, Shape, and swimsuit magazines offer some good examples. Also, I'd suggest wearing some nice thongs, sun glasses, or unusual hat. The idea is to create that refined look and not to look like a bum.

Your most important item to bring with you is your ice chest. Stock it with an assortment of liquor. I'd suggest some beer, wine, coke, and pre-made mixed drinks that come in cans you can purchase at your local liquor store. Don't forget the plastic bar glasses! Also bring your inflatable air mattress and an extra one if possible, and a good-sounding radio.

OK, now you're looking the part and you've got all your attraction ammunition with you. Let's take it step by step using these proven techniques:

You've entered the pool area. Make a complete circle around the pool to check out the available men. While walking and you catch the eye of a male, instantly remark, "Hi" or "Hello" or "It sure is a pretty day isn't it?" If you get a response, keep walking and make a circle and come back to him. When you return ask him, "Can I join you?" Most likely he won't mind. Introduce yourself and offer him a drink. Turn on your radio and ask him if there's any particular station he would like to listen to. To establish some physical contact, ask him to rub some sun tan oil on your back. If you've played your cards right and turned on your charm and conversational skills, you should be on your way.

Another technique to use is what I call the old "air mattress technique." Here is how it works: Sit your ice chest on the edge of the pool to where you have access to it while laying on your

FINDING MR. RIGHT

air mattress. Now, get on your air mattress with a can of beer or mixed drink in hand (I might add that it would be a good idea to try and keep your hair dry. This way you'll look more attractive. A person with wet hair is not very eye-appealing). Maneuver your air mattress around the pool and park it across from a male near the pool. Then just simply remark, "You sure are getting a nice tan today." This breaks the ice and then follow up with, "I've got an extra air mattress. Would you like to join me?" This technique will really work for you successfully and I highly recommend that you try it. Also, if there are other males in the pool on air mattresses, pull up beside them and feed them the same opening lines.

Tours

This is an excellent way to meet male tourists and these tours have some lonely attractive males.

Every major city has walking or bus tours. Cities on the water usually have boat tours of some type. Check the yellow pages under "tours" to find out information on the tours. Sign up for one of the tours on the weekend.

Meeting these men on a tour is easy as pie. All you've got to do for openers is to make a comment on what the tour guide is showing you. Also, it would be a good idea to bring a polaroid camera along with you so you can take a picture of him to take back home with him.

After the tour is completed, ask him if you can take him on a personal guided tour of some unique places in the city. Being that you live there, I'm sure you can think of some great places to take him.

So why not try this method of meeting men. It's a uniquely different way of meeting men and some of the tours are very interesting. The atmosphere is great and the people are relaxed and friendly.

Theater Groups

Large metropolitan areas have numerous amateur theater

Where to Meet Men

groups. They can also be found in small communities. These groups are full of nice men. Backstage romances are very common.

Contact one of these groups and volunteer your services. If you act or feel like you could act, try and land a part. If possible, try to select a part where you will kiss or hug an actor. A professional actor wouldn't take these things to heart but a smalltown guy will get off on them. Your reward, of course, comes when he accepts an invitation to your home to "rehearse."

If you don't care to act, there are plenty of activities you can participate in such as prop, stage hand, set designer, advertising, ticket taker, etc. Take anything, even if it's cleanup. The main objective is participation.

You'll be working with the crew and will be spending a lot of time together. You'll become close and you will feel like one big family. This leaves the door open to intimate relationships with the opposite sex.

Another advantage to working with a theater group is that you will be participating in a lot of social activities. There will be backstage get-togethers and lots of parties. These are golden opportunities for meeting the men.

Look into this way of meeting men. It will be a lot of fun and increase your circle of friends.

Friends and Relatives

This is an ideal way to meet men. Just make a list of all your friends and relatives. Then contact them by phone or in person and ask them if they know of any single men they could introduce you to. It's nothing to be embarrassed about when asking. You're just wanting some male companionship.

Meeting men this way is very natural and your friend or relative can usually tell you a lot about the man. Some will really enjoy playing the role of cupid. Who knows, you may meet the love of your life, just by asking around.

FINDING MR. RIGHT

At Work

Take a real good look around you when you're at work. Depending on how large of company you work for and what type of work you do, you're going to see a lot of eligible men. Don't pass up the opportunities to meet men. You can make a lot of social contacts, being that you spend a lot of your time at work.

At a very large company you may actually have anywhere from a hundred to a thousand men to choose from. Talk about heaven on earth! Places of employment are hot beds for romance and behind the scenes activities.

How do you approach men at work? Just introduce yourself. Say, "Hi, my name is _____. I work in the _____ dept. Being that we work for the same company, I thought I'd introduce myself." Then carry on a conversation from there. Don't forget to charm and compliment him. After you've gotten to know him and established some rapport, ask him out to lunch. Who knows, that could lead to an intimate relationship.

A word about any new men at work. Be sure and hit up on them right away. Don't let the other women beat you to the punch. Welcome him to the company and try and make him feel at home. Introduce him to your coworkers. Invite him to join your lunch group for something to eat.

Finally, don't pass up any company parties, picnics, trips, bowling or softball leagues, banquets, etc. These are great for meeting and mingling with your male co-workers.

The Beach

This is one of the more favorable and popular spots to meet men. They are there for the taking. Take your pick! The beach provides a perfect setting for meeting men. It's a casual and relaxed atmosphere and most of the men are friendly. It's just simply a matter of approaching them and talking to them. That's all there is to it.

A lot of girls make the mistake of going to the beach and

Where to Meet Men

just stare at men and they stroll up and down the beach not even smiling or saying, "Hi" to men as they walk along. They don't even stop to talk to a man that catches their eye. They just don't have the guts to approach them. What's really sad is that these men are there to have a good time and attract the opposite sex. Why do you think they are so tan and have a nice muscular body. It's to turn you on.

So be bold and you'll be surprised how easy it is to meet men at the beach.

Now, I will describe some important techniques and strategies to use at the beach. Use them and you can't fail and you will have the summer of your life!

It's important how you dress for the beach. Dress well and don't just wear a pair of old cut-offs with holes in them. Wear a nice designer bathing suit like you see in Cosmo, Shape, or swimsuit magazines. Also, while not sunning, wear a shirt appropriate for the beach such as a tank top or colorful T-shirt. Invest in some nice attractive sunglasses (not the cheap kind). Try on several different styles and select the one that makes you look unique and different.

Now, you'll be all decked out for the beach and you'll stand out from the rest of the ordinary girls. What this means is that you'll attract the attention of the opposite sex and that's what you're striving for.

You should bring some very important equipment that you'll use in meeting men. These are as follows:

1. ICE CHEST - This is your most important item. Fill it with beer, wine, mixed drinks in a can, and soft drinks. You'll use this to offer a man a drink when you've approached a man.

2. BLANKET - Bring a blanket big enough for you and a man to lay on. Make sure it's clean and attractive and not old and smelly.

3. FRISBEE, VOLLEYBALL, BEACHBALL, FOOTBALL With these you can approach a man and ask, "Want to play?"

4. RADIO - This comes in handy. What to do is lay near a man or group of men and turn on your radio. Then I'll ask, "What station would you like to hear?" This opens the door for further conversation.

FINDING MR. RIGHT

5. BODY SURFING BOARD - Buy two of them. They are cheap and made of styrofoam. Approach a man and ask him if he'd like to do some body surfing.

6. SURFBOARD - If you do surf this can be an advantage. Some men are very attracted to surfers. Most men don't know how to surf and have never even been on a surfboard. If you do surf, all you have to do is approach a man and ask him, "Would you like to learn how to surf?" If you don't know how to surf yourself you can always fake it. It will be a lot of fun trying anyway.

7. SUN TAN OIL - Here's one that will always work. Approach a man and ask him, "Would you rub some sun tan oil on my back?" You'll never get turned down and it really feels good having a man rubbing your back.

While walking the beach looking for men, when a guy catches your eye, give him a warm smile and say, "Hi." If he responds, don't keep walking whatever you do. Stop immediately and start talking to him. Invite him over to your blanket and offer him something to drink or you can invite him to go in the water. Also you can ask him if he wants to play some beach sports such as frisbee, volleyball, beachball, etc.

If you pass a man that you're interested in and he has his eyes closed, just approach him and say, "Weren't you on the cover of Gentleman's Quarterly?" He will be flattered and this opens up a conversation.

In conclusion, I hope I've given you some new ideas you have never thought of before on how to meet men at the beach. Happy hunting!

Adult Education Classes and University Extension Courses

Most good-sized communities in the United States offer adult education courses. The courses are varied and offer something for everyone. The classes are held at convenient times for full time workers and are available at no cost or for a small fee.

These courses are an excellent channel for meeting men.

Where to Meet Men

The key to it all is to take courses that appeal to men. Let me offer some suggestions of courses that will be made up of mostly men: car mechanics, golf, racquetball, business, investing, photography, etc. By taking these courses you will be one of the few females in the class. You will be surrounded by men and you will get all the attention and you will be in demand. The men will be literally fighting amongst themselves for your attention.

Let me tell you about my friend Gail who took a automechanics class at my urging. This is what she told me about the class: "Well, there were fifteen men in the class and I was the only female. Most of them were single and most of them were around my age. Now, I've only been to three of the classes and have three more to go and I've already dated four of the men...and I'm becoming a great mechanic on top of it. You know Don, this was a really great idea of yours. Probably none of these men would have talked to me if I had approached them in a supermarket or on the subway, but no man refuses to talk to you over an automobile."

A word of advice. Arrive at the classes early. Everyone sits around and shoots the bull and the atmosphere is very relaxed and there's no pressure to meet someone like in a singles bar. By arriving early you can make the rounds and converse with the men before class.

Male Strip Joints

I sincerely hope you're not one of those women who go to strip joints just to watch the male dancers. Most women do and they don't know what they are missing out on. These men can be picked up and are generally easy to meet. A lot of women don't even try to pick them up and it's a shame because these men need lovin just like any other man.

How do you approach these men? Well, normally they will be approaching you possibly to hustle you for drinks. Don't hold this against them and think they're just trying to take you for a ride. They're just trying to make a living and they get a

FINDING MR. RIGHT

commission on these drinks.

You might as well face the facts that you just might have to buy them a drink to talk to them. These can be house rules. Buy them a drink or two, it won't kill you. Just be nice to them and treat them with respect and you can get somewhere with them.

OK, let's say you've bought a dancer a drink and he's sitting with you (possibly on your lap kissing you). Turn on your charm and conversational skills at this point. Ask him if he'd like to go out for breakfast when he gets off. This will usually be after hours. If he declines, don't let this discourage you. He may have other plans or may just not feel like it. Then ask him if he'd like to go out to dinner on his day off. And by all means ask him if you could give him a call sometimes. You'd really be surprised how easy they are to date and they are very friendly.

You're going to run into the type that are very wild and promiscuous. They will screw anything in sight. Also, you may run into a dancer that is supporting a drug habit. You will meet all kinds and most of them are real nice men that you would enjoy dating.

Make it a point to pick out a strip joint and go there regularly at the same time and the same day of the week. You will usually see the same dancers. You'll become a familiar face and become friends with all the dancers. There's a lot of competition sometimes among the dancers for the girlfriends of the other dancers. They will actually try to steal each others girlfriends away from each other. Wouldn't you like to have a bunch of handsome exotic dancers fighting over you? Talk about heaven!

A word about spending money. Don't throw it around trying to impress the men, especially if you can't afford it. They are use to this and it doesn't impress them that much. When they keep pressuring you for drinks and you want to stop buying them drinks, just explain to him that you know the ropes of his business and you'd rather spend your money on him away from the club. He will understand.

Another method of meeting them and getting them to leave

Where to Meet Men

with you is to try and offer them some drugs, especially cocaine. Some of them do drugs and some would do "anything" for drugs. In conclusion, don't sit around and drool and stare at these men anymore. Make an effort to meet and attract these men. Don't beat around the bush with them. Just come right out and tell him that you want to see him when he's off work.

Nudist Parks, Clubs, Beaches, and Resorts

Here you have an advantage, in that you get to see the man that you want to approach in the nude.

These type of places contain men and some of them single. Of course, there are a lot of couples also. Most nudist resorts are open to single female memberships.

You may be saying to yourself, "Where are all these places?" Well, I'll be providing you complete information for contacting these places. Everything you'll need to know to get started.

Nudist clubs and resorts can be contacted by letter or phone. Just tell them that you are considering joining their club and would like to come as a visitor. They will provide you with complete details and directions and will personally meet you at the gate to take you on a free tour.

Currently there are over 200 of these nudist parks and resorts and over 100,000 nudists in the U.S.

About nude beaches. You'll find some great guys here with nice bodies. However, just because he's there doesn't mean he's and easy catch. Some are just sun worshipers. Just treat him with respect and you should not have any problems.

There are many nude beaches in the U.S. and they are not legal but they are tolerated by the local authorities. At the end of this section, you'll find listed, a company under the heading of Additional Sources that has complete information on locations of nude beaches. Write them.

Here's a listing of four of the most popular nudists resorts in the U.S. Please call or write these locations first because you never know when they may run into legal problems.

FINDING MR. RIGHT

Treehouse Fun Ranch
17809 Glen Helen Rd.
San Bernardino, CA 92407
Telephone: (714) 887-3110 or (714) 887-3491
   Average age under 30. Families come here as well as couples and singles. The General public is welcome at almost all of the special events, and the cost is usually from $5 to $10.

Sandstone
21400 Saddlepeak Rd.
Topanga, CA 90290
Telephone: (213) 455-9055 or (213) 455-2530
   Open sexuality is the norm. Lots of swinging and sex practiced out in the open. The Sandstone philosophy is, "we believe in casual affairs, but we're into loving also. We make friends here, and we care about people." Inquire about "singles" night which is usually a weekend night.

Sunshine Park
Somers Point Rd.
May's Landing, NJ 08330
Telephone: (609) 625-1357 or (609) 625-2486
   Today the Park is the biggest nude resort in the northeastern part of the United States, and one of the most progressive also. The people are of all ages but the majority are young adults. Sex is private between consenting adults. There is swinging but it is done very discreetly. This park is noted for very attractive girls. There is usually a quota system in effect for the number of single men they will let in.

The Four Seasons
Freelton, Ontario CANADA
Telephone: (416) 659-7784
   This is the Holiday Inn of Canadian nude resorts. There's a mixed crowd. There are families and children here, and also a lot of single couples. The Four Seasons is about forty-five minutes from downtown Toronto, near Hamilton.

Where to Meet Men

Additional Sources

Fun Club
Box 428
Bellflower, CA 90706

This company has the most comprehensive and extensive information of nudist clubs, resorts, and beaches. Send for details. Here's some of the information available:

Nudist Publications

1. "Nude Beaches of California" complete with maps.
2. "Naked Beach" - About the largest nude beach area in the world!
3. "Bare in Mind" monthly nudist newspaper.
4. "Hot Springs and Pools of the Southwest" - Complete illustrated guide.
5. "The Nude Beach" book - Everything you want to know...
6. "Guide to American Nudist Resorts" complete with maps.

Nudist Information Sheets

1. 53 U.S. Clothing Optional Groups.
2. 18 U.S. Clothing Optional Beaches.
3. 78 Overseas Clothing Optional Beaches.
4. How to Visit Nudist Parks, Clubs, Beaches, and Resorts.
5. Nudist Parks, Clubs, and Resorts - Eastern U.S., Central U.S., Western U.S., and overseas.

In conclusion, I'd recommend buying the book, "World Guide to Nude Beaches and Recreation", by Lee Baxandall. Published by Stonehill, 212 pages, illustrated, $10.95.

This is a gazetteer of "free" beaches. There is a special section devoted to the Caribbean islands where toplessness and bottomlessness are catching on - or taking off. The guide is profusely illustrated with more colored photos of happy nudies than are perhaps absolutely necessary to make the point. But

FINDING MR. RIGHT

why complain?

Also, I'd recommend buying the book, "Nude Beaches and Resorts from the Fun Club, as well as the Fun Club Information Sheets numbers 7,8,10,11,12 and 13 so that you have locations of representative nudist beaches, parks, clubs and resorts in your area.

CHAPTER THREE

Dating Services

These include computer dating, video dating, and dating referral services. These can be expensive but are well worth it. Besides, look at all the money you can drink away in bars.

These services area very dignified and respectable way to meet members of the opposite sex. Your results are going to depend largely on the individual service. Try and select a service with the largest number of persons in the computer, largest number of clientele, and the largest video service. This way you'll have a wider selection and better choice of men.

Don't make the mistake a friend of mine did in choosing a small dating service that was only in business four months. They only had a few men to match her up with and those were disappointing and weren't the type of men she was looking for.

Another tip of advice. When you use these services, don't depend on them to contact you to find a mate. You've got to call them and bug the hell out of them to keep the dates coming. Otherwise, after you've paid your fee, they may forget about you. Some services are overloaded with clients and understaffed

FINDING MR. RIGHT

and will forget about you unless you call them frequently.
Now I will describe how these services work:

Computer Dating

There are two versions. Local and computer dating done by mail.

Here's how the mail version works. You fill out a personality profile which is designed to match you to members of the opposite sex who (a) share your interests, (b) compliment your personality, and (c) suit your tastes.

When they receive your personality profile, it is programmed into the computer. The computer analyzes your data and locates the type of people you would like to date. The computer then chooses your date...selecting people that are likely to be "in tune" with you. You are matched to people from your area. Your personality profile is used to select people who meet your objectives and interests, and compliment your personality.

Each month, you receive your exclusive computer preview of your dates. You receive the name, address and telephone number of your dates, plus helpful information to make that first meeting with the opposite sex go smoothly and pleasantly. Your computer preview is just the thing to help you receive at least two new dates each month for 12 months. The companies usually cost around $50 -100 annually.

If you're interested in contacting one of these companies, let me recommend one: Comdates, telephone (414) 782-9194. Ask them to mail you details on their dating service. Check your Yellow Pages for listings of others.

The other version is your local computer dating service. You will fill out a personality profile and will be interviewed by their staff (usually has a psychology background). You will be thoroughly screened to insure the high basic standards you require. A computer will be used for "final" matching. Then you will be given the phone number of your match and then you just simply call him and arrange a meeting.

Dating Services

A word of advice when you set up a meeting. Don't put the man to the expense of a dinner and a movie and a night on the town. Just simply meet somewhere for a drink that's quiet. Meeting for lunch is even better. This is just an initial meeting to determine if you would like each other and would want to see each other again. So, don't have the guy blow $50 on you and you may not even like the guy. After you meet, you should know whether you want to see each other again.

Dating Referral Services

These are similar to computer dating except they don't use computers. The matches are hand picked. You will fill out a detailed personality profile and will be matched with this and according to your looks. If you are an attractive woman, you certainly won't get matched up with a man that's fat and ugly. You will be given the phone number of your match and you'll take it from there.

You'll probably be given at least two phone numbers per week. The cost of these services? They usually start out at about $200 for six months. That's $33 per month. You can blow that much in one night on your self in a bar.

These services are also offered by mail nationally. The largest and most prominent one is called Dateline (TOLL FREE 1-800-727-3300). Also, there is Christian Singles(TOLL FREE 1-800-323-8113), Playmates International, telephone (717) 848-1408. Call these services and request a brochure.

Video Dating

This is probably the most innovative way for single people to meet each other today.

Rather than wasting their valuable time and money looking for more compatible partners, the video dating members have unique benefits not available to the general public. Among them are:

FINDING MR. RIGHT

* All members can see and hear color videotapes of all other members before they meet; this removes the blindness from dating.
* All members can choose for themselves who they wish to meet.
* Full names and telephone numbers are exchanged only when there is mutual consent.
* Nobody matchmakes for the members; they choose for themselves.

What's really unique about video dating is that you'll know more about a person you've chosen to meet than you would in a blind situation, answering personal ads, or even someone face to face at a party or singles bar.

The cost? Generally $30-40 a month. in reality it's really free because with all the free dinners, entertainment expenses, etc. that the men pay for that you meet, will more than make up for your fee.

How does video dating work? You will be carefully screened, interviewed, fill out a personality profile, have a photo taken, and be interviewed on video tape.

What does being videotaped involve? The videotaping process is really quite simple. Beforehand, you and one of the staff members will review the kinds of subjects that the two of you will talk about: your calling, career, your goals in life, hobbies, interests, activities that you enjoy, and any social requirements, restrictions, or preferences you might have in a man.

Some people find it helpful to jot down in advance any special points they'd like the interviewer to cover during the taping. Others prefer to just let the conversation happen spontaneously. The actual videotaping only takes a few minutes, and nearly everyone admits that it was easier to do than they had imagined.

Let me stress that the video you make is critical to your success in video dating. You will be judged by the way you look, act, and express yourself. Be sure and look your best and try to

Dating Services

act natural and not nervous. I'd recommend taking a tranquilizer before taping or have a glass of wine if you think that you will be tense and nervous. Just remember to smile and laugh a lot while taping. This will make a favorable impression on the men that will be viewing your tape.

Also, a word about the personality profile you will be filling out. This will consist of what you like to do, what kind of person you are, and what you're looking for. Just keep it simple and don't make the mistake of coming on too strong. As you know, a lot of men are afraid of commitment and you'll scare them away saying that you're looking for marriage. Keep it clean, too, and don't write with sexual overtones.

Also, photos will be required to go with your profile. Unfortunately, you will be judged on how you look in your photos. Some men will select women just on the basis of their good looks. So use the best photos you have available. I'd strongly recommend having some made in a portrait studio.

Let me explain how the selection process works. You will look thru the personality profiles of their male members (they are usually arranged in alphabetical order). Their photos will also be with their profile, so you will see what they look like.

All you do is simply select your choices (you're usually allowed 10-12 selections per month). On the profile sheet the member has a code number that corresponds with his tape in the video tape library. Then you view the tapes and make your final selections. Then the males that you select will be notified and they will come in and look at your profile and view your tape. If he is interested, he will be given your phone number and also you will be given his phone number. So you just call each other up and take it from there.

So why not check this out. I don't think you will be disappointed. The clientele are hard-working, professional single adults who couldn't (or wouldn't) waste the time, energy and money taken up with the "dating game" in bars, blind dates, or chance encounters.

There's no guarantee that you'll meet Mr. Right but you'll certainly be socially active. Sure beats sitting at home not meeting any men at all!

CHAPTER FOUR

How to Meet Men Using Personal Ads

This section is devoted to the highly effective way of meeting men by answering and running personal classified ads in national and local singles publications. Many women have used this method and get stacks of letters (with photos) from nice men from all over the United States and locally.

There's lots of lonely men out there searching for romance and companionship. Advertising is a dignified way for them to meet women and they are able to screen the women that respond through their letters, photos, and phone calls.

There's only going to be one drawback to this method unless you meet someone local. You will probably have to do some traveling to meet the men. However, most men will go to the expense to visit you first. A lot of people have found their life mate this way. If you like to travel, you can travel all over the United States, meeting men you've become intimate with thru correspondence and talking over the phone. Also, a lot of men are willing to pay all your expenses to come visit them. What a great way for a free vacation!

FINDING MR. RIGHT

How to Get Men to Write You First

This involves running a good pulling ad in the several good national publications. Always keep at least one ad running at all times. That way your mailbox will always be full of letters and photos from these nice men.

Let's talk about running a good ad that will "pull." Whatever you do, don't publish a short ad with basic information about yourself. This won't work and you'll receive very few replies from such an uninteresting and plain, dull ad.

Your ad's got to appeal to men. You've got to convince him that you're not the average woman and have a lot to offer him. You've got to offer him something he can't get from the average woman. You've really got to interest him to answer your ad.

Here an example of a national ad that was very successful for a friend of mine:

I LOVE YOU DARLING! How long have you longed to hear these words? How often have you longed to hold in your arms, a woman who is affectionate and loving - to be cuddled, caressed and kissed, warmly, sweetly, tenderly? Perhaps you are my sweetheart - who knows? Nice, attractive one-man woman, writer, 34, 5'5", 110 lbs., desires to meet attractive, loving, slender man 25-40 who is interested in a meaningful relationship leading to marriage. Photo please.

In summation, include these items in your ad:
1. Occupation.
2. Age, height, and weight.
3. What you're looking for in a man.

The following are some good-pulling ads that have run in some local publications:

This is my favorite! Just run this ad and edit it to fit your description. You will get a lot of replies!

How to Meet Men Using Personal Ads

Single female 1953 model, low mileage, high performance. Bumped a few times, but never wrecked. Proven ability to hug the road and not wander off course. Exterior in mint condition, warm, sentimental, sensitive interior, never soiled. Factory equipped entertainment package includes stereo, humor, depth, imagination and intelligence. Radio picks up all kinds of rock and jazz. Spacious seats with plenty of room for passenger...runs on high-octane fun and romance, lifetime supply included. Available for inspection by male drivers only, prefer 25-45 eye-catching exterior, self-confident, non-materialistic, warm, sincere with sense of humor and full set of tools. Come from close solid family, would like to have little Toyotas some day. Equipped with Marketing Degree. Only driven once a week by little old lady to/from church. To arrange test drive, please write. HAPPY MOTORING.

SWF, 34, very pretty, slender hot potato, recently dropped (vocation - mistress), needs to be rescued by unattached male who needs permanent outside diversion. No monetary obligation.

SWF, 24, very pretty, slender Catholic needs mature church-going male (25-45, handsome, slender) for lasting and loving relationship. Must be into group functions, wafers, and early morning mass.

SWF, 28, very pretty, slender, who flunked Disco and Bars 101, seeking handsome, slender, affectionate male (25-45), for the usual reasons.

SWF, very pretty, affectionate, petite , 25, need male companionship (25-45, handsome slender) for going to movies, dancing, warm friendship and finishing all my leftovers.

DWF, 34, nice-looking, slender, would like to meet male of same marital status (25-45, handsome, slender) for "war story" exchange and soothing battle scars.

FINDING MR. RIGHT

Final tip. Don't list your name, address, or phone number in an ad. This will give the impression that you're desperate and undesirable.

Here's a list of good national publications containing singles ads:

Singles "Critique"
Box 5062
Sherman Oaks, CA 91413
  Write and request sample copy and enclose $1. The publication is available at most major hotels in large cities.

Electronic Exchange
Box 68
Manhattan Beach, CA 90266
  Meet men for sports, hobbies, workouts, vacations, travel, correspondence for any purpose. Members throughout the United States and over eighty other countries. Wide range of interests. Privacy assured. Small cost. Write for free information.

National Singles Register
Box 567
Norwalk, CA 90650
  Write and request a sample copy and enclose $1. This publication is available at most major motels in large cities.

Sheela Wood - GLOBE magazine
Box 3890
New York, NY 10163
  Available everywhere. Published weekly and a real good puller for running ads. Large circulation. Lots of men read this publication.

Sheela Wood - THE EXAMINER magazine
Box 32
Rouses Point, NY 12979-0032
  Available everywhere. Published weekly and also a real good

How to Meet Men Using Personal Ads

puller for running ads, but not as good as the GLOBE.

Country Style Magazine
11058 W. Addison St.
Franklin Park, IL 60131
   Available at most newsstands. Accepts personal ads in the classified section.

Latin International
Box 1716
Chula Vista, CA 92012
   Write for information to get your photo published with a profile.

Cupid's Destiny
Box 5637
Reno, NV 89514
   Published since 1937. Send $1 for sample copy which will contain subscription details.

Western Heart
2309 E. Main St.
Mesa, AZ 85203
   Published since 1926. Write for free descriptive literature.

Sheela Wood - THE SUN magazine
Box 33
Rouses Point, NY 12979-0033
   Available at most newsstands. Published weekly and a good puller for running ads.

R.L. Moore
Englewood, FL 34295-1264
   Write and request to get listed in their publication, PHOTO WORLD.

FINDING MR. RIGHT

Family Travel Log
People Pleasers
Box 406
Kewanee, IL 61443-0406
  Write for details on getting listed free in their People Pleasers section.

Playtime International   Nice Personals
Box 3355   Box 345
York, PA 17402   Kenilworth, IL 60043

Singles Life   Personals, Inc.
1430 Elliot Ave. W.   Box 26139
Seattle, WA 98119   Fairview Park, OH 44126

   Lastly, it can take up to two months (depending on the publication) before you will start receiving letters and photos in response to your ad.

When the Man Answers Your Ad

   The main objective in responding to his letter is to make a good impression on him.
   Your letter is going to be selling yourself to him. Don't write back on cheap ordinary writing paper.
   You've got to use first class elegant stationary. Have some nice "personalized stationary" with envelopes printed up by your local printer. Ivory and blue colors look real nice. If you want to order some real nice looking stationary, write this company and request a free catalog. Here's the address: The Drawing Board, Box 220505, Dallas, TX 75222. They are very reasonable and have a wide selection.
   If you have illegible handwriting, you'll make a better impression by typing the letter. "Script" style of type looks real nice. If you don't type, you can hire a secretarial service to type it out for you.
   If you have ivory paper, write it in brown or green ink. This

How to Meet Men Using Personal Ads

looks real nice.

When replying to his letter, you can enclose him a stamp to write you back with. This is good courtesy and is very thoughtful.

Your Letter

Here's an sample letter a friend of mine used to write back the men that answered her national ads. This letter was very successful and she got a lot of positive responses with it. Modify it to fit your situation.

Mr. Derick Evans
2201 Nathaniel
Los Angeles, CA 90075

Dear Derick:

Thank you for answering my ad in "Globe Magazine." I really appreciated your handsome photo. On the basis of your "sweet" letter and photo, I've come to the conclusion that you are a very nice person and the type of man I've been looking for. I sincerely hope we get a chance to meet, for I feel that a man like you could make my life happy in many ways. My main goal in life at this time is to meet an unmarried and unattached man who is sincerely interested in marriage to a one-man woman. I'm not concerned about your religion or economic status as these things are unimportant to me. What's important to me is your truthfulness, honesty, and loyalty. If married to me, you would not have to work if you didn't want to. However, if you did want to work I would prefer that you help me with my publishing business. All this would consist of would be filling orders for books during your leisure hours at home. Again, you would not be required to work because I have enough earning power and education for the both of us. If married to you, I will share all the wealth I've accumulated in the past and future on an equal basis. As my husband, lover and friend, everything is half yours and I'm a very unselfish person.

FINDING MR. RIGHT

I'm white, single, educated, refined, generous, well-informed on all subjects, intelligent, very attractive (been told many times that I look like a model), well-groomed, and have a good sense of humor. I know how to treat a man and I could satisfy and fulfill your needs like you've never experienced before. I'm extremely affectionate and very romantic. I love candlelight dinners, fireplaces, holding hands, walking hand in hand along the beach at sunset, and bubblebaths. Also, I love to shower the "man in my life" with lots of kisses and tokens of affection such as flowers, cards, gifts, etc.

I will accept you as you are and would not try to change you. I think it's very important for a man to be "himself." I would want to expand your life and not try to suppress it in any manner. I'm not the jealous, domineering, and possessive type at all. If married to me you would remain independent and could pursue and enjoy all the activities that you enjoy. Also, if married to me you would know of my whereabouts and what I was doing at all times. I love traveling and take many long trips. As my husband you would become my traveling companion. I have been in 36 states and 26 foreign countries. There's nothing I wouldn't enjoy more than seeing interesting places with the man I love.

I'm very modern woman in all respects and very up-to-date with the times. I don't live in the past and live one day at a time with a positive outlook.

My leisure activities include mountain-climbing, canoeing, kayaking, fishing, camping, hiking, bowling, playing the organ and guitar, and all sports. Also, I enjoy eating out, good music of all kinds, live theatre, reading, going to movies, and good conversation.

I'm very mature and well-established and financially secure. You would never have to worry about money or financial security if married to me. Your physical looks are not of the utmost importance to me. I'm more interested in "inner beauty." I'll take a warm-hearted plain-looking man any day over a handsome man with a cold heart. I'll have to admit that it is nice to have a very handsome man to look at, but physical

How to Meet Men Using Personal Ads

beauty is an attribute that fades with age, giving way to wrinkles and added weight.

In case you're wondering why I answered your ad. Well it can be summed up in Johnny Lee's hit song, "Looking For Love in All the Wrong Places." In the past I've gone to nightclubs to meet the opposite sex. All I've gotten out of this is shallow relationships and the all too common, "one night stand." The men I meet don't seem to be interested in a meaningful relationship. They just want to play the field. I just can't handle all the game playing in clubs. That's why I wrote you. At least I know you're looking for a meaningful relationship and someone to love just as I am.

I'm very easygoing and easy to please. I also believe in sharing responsibilities on an equal basis. I love to cook. I'd share domestic chores with you and I'm no perfectionist when it comes to housecleaning.

I must be totally honest with you and tell you that I consider sex very important in marriage. I have a strong, passionate, and healthy sex drive. It would be important to me that you have a healthy attitude towards sex and have a desire to keep your wife satisfied and fulfilled in this important area. Concerning children, if you desired to have children, that would be OK with me. If you didn't desire to have children that would be OK also. I'd be happy with you with or without children.

If you're still interested, Derick, I would like to hear from you again real soon. At the bottom of this letter you will find my home and business phone numbers. Feel free to call me anytime. Please tell me about yourself, the things you enjoy, your goals in life, and anything you have strong feelings about. This would be helpful to evaluate the things we have in common and if we could get along in a close relationship (marriage).

I have a lot to offer you as a wife, lover, and friend and if you're interested, I would like for us to meet and spend some time together to determine if we are compatible and if we could become deeply involved in a relationship. If this worked out favorably and we hit it off real well, I would favor us getting married soon. Being that distance separates us, it would be difficult to have a long courtship involving numerous trips and dates. A conventional courtship would definitely be out of the question.

So if you're disappointed and tired of what you've had up till now and want to settle down, and ready for a first-class woman to come into your life and treat you like a King and fill your life with love and happiness, please write or call me without further delay. If you can recognize a truly sincere letter, then you'll know that this is "the real thing."

Sincerely,

You Write the Men First

All you do is read thru the personal ads and circle the ones that appeal to you. Then you will answer with your printed form letter.

This is a quick way to get those letters and photos to start coming in. You don't even have to wait for any ads to break.

You're going to be using a printed form letter rather than answering letters by hand. Writing letters would be too time consuming.

A lot of these men are sincerely interested in a meaningful relationship. A lot of them live in remote areas where there aren't too many eligible women to choose from. Of course there's the type out there that are just looking for a free meal ticket and a rich woman. But, most of them are sincere and nice men.

Some words of advice. Don't answer ads where they don't list their weight. They are usually overweight. If obesity doesn't bother you, then answer anyway. Also, if no age is listed they are usually too old for you. Stay away from recently divorced men also. They are a poor prospect for a relationship due to their emotionally unstable state of mind.

About all the printed form letters. Those used successfully

How to Meet Men Using Personal Ads

will be described at the end of this section. Type these letters up or have them typed by a secretarial service and take them to your local print shop. Have about 100 copies made. These will be done by camera so they will look professional. Don't have them zeroxed! Also, your letters could be produced on a computer with a letter-quality printer.

OK, now you're ready to answer an ad. Don't send a photo to a blind ad. They are expensive and some will not answer your letter back and you'll be minus a photo. Don't send a photo until he writes you a nice encouraging letter containing his photo. Then send him one. There's one exception concerning photos. If you are attractive, I'd recommend sending a photo initially. This will increase your chances of him responding. This option is up to you.

Follow the publications directions carefully when answering ads. It usually takes 3 to 5 weeks to receive answers from the men running ads in national publications.

Here's a sample form letter used when answering national ads:

Hi!

I LOVE YOU DARLING! How often have you longed to hear these words? How often have you longed to held in the arms of a woman who is affectionate and loving to be cuddled, caressed and kissed, warmly, sweetly, tenderly? Perhaps you are my sweetheart - who knows?

This letter is in response to your recent "personal" ad.

I'm 5'6", 118 lbs. Professionally I'm a writer, published author, professional astrologer, and own my own publishing company. Also, I've been an industrial lab technician for over 14 years. As you can tell, I'm very ambitious and one of my main goals in life is to become financially, independent. I am now and have been taking steps to fulfill that goal.

I desire to meet an unmarried and unattached man who is sincerely interested in marriage to a one-man woman. Your religion and economic status are really not important to me.

FINDING MR. RIGHT

Your honesty, truthfulness, and loyalty are of utmost importance to me. If married to me you could pursue your own career, but if for some reason you didn't want to I would prefer that you help me run our business operations, but again this would not be required if you didn't want to. If married to you, I would, of course, share what I've accumulated in the past, plus what I earn and accumulate in the future on an equal basis with you. I'm a very unselfish person and as my husband, lover and "lifetime" companion I would truly consider everything half yours. I'm white (German, French, and Irish), educated, intelligent, well-informed, good sense of humor, clean, neat dresser, beautiful teeth, age 35 (look much younger), very attractive (been told many times that I look like a model), extremely affectionate and romantic, refined and generous. I'm modern up-to-date and in-step with the times, and not trying to re-live or hold on to the past.

I do not smoke but have no objections to the man in my life smoking. It is important to me that he "be himself," so I have no desire to try and take away any of those things that you already have that are valuable and important to you. I would want to enhance and expand your life, and not suppress it in any manner. This is what love is all about. I would want you happy as my spouse and I feel that those things I advocate here would be necessary for total happiness. I'm not the jealous type of person. If married to me you certainly would not lose your independence, and therefore you could "be yourself" and pursue those activities in which you are interested.

All the things I like to do for recreation, I like to do them with the "man in my life." I drink an occasional mixed drink and I enjoy two or three drinks in the evening when out with my lover. If married to me you would know of my whereabouts and what I was doing at all times.

I have two nice color TV'S in my home, but seldom ever turn them on. The normal shows on TV bore me to death. I prefer reading when at home in the evening unless there's a good "special" on TV or sports. I keep up with current events by reading the paper and listening to radio news. I very much enjoy

How to Meet Men Using Personal Ads

going on long trips to interesting places and doing interesting things with the man in my life. I have been in 36 states and 16 foreign countries.

I am not interested in "one night stands" with men. I could never exploit and use men in this manner, knowing full well that I had no future to offer them. Sweet and nice men are too "precious" to me for me to ever exploit and use them. I'm looking for a meaningful and lasting relationship with one man that will lead to early marriage.

I'm mature and well-established. Your financial security would be assured. Your age is unimportant to me if you are sincere, and mature in your thinking. As you know, age does not always denote the degree of maturity in one's thinking. Your physical looks are not of primary importance to me as long as you're clean and neat in appearance. While it is nice to have someone who is handsome to look at, physical beauty is a fleeting thing and fades with age, invariably giving way to "father time." I'm far more interested in "inner beauty", love, respect and admiration for each other that is not affected by time, and can and should last forever.

My leisure activities include mountain-climbing, canoeing, kayaking, fishing, camping, hiking, bowling, playing the organ and guitar, and all sports. I might add that I am a fitness nut also. Also, I enjoy dining out, good music of all kinds, love to dance, live theatre, reading, going to the movies and good conversation.

I love candlelight dinners, fireplaces, holding hands while walking along the beach at sunset, bubblebaths, and giving back rubs. Also, I love to shower "the man in my life" with lots of kisses and tokens of affection such as flowers, cards, gifts, etc.

I'm as down-to-earth as an "old shoe", so please realize that what I need from you is certainly nothing complicated. I realize that all of the desirable characteristics, traits and talents will never be found all combined in one man. Neither will they all be found in one woman. We all have our faults, and to me the sensible thing to do is decide what is important to us in our partner, and when we find these things be ready to accept our good fortune, and be ready to accept and be happy with those shortcomings that are of lesser importance.

I'm no fanatic on housekeeping, and when married I try to share these chores on somewhat of a 50-50 basis with my spouse, because afterall, I live there too.

It is important to me that my husband, lover and companion try to be a good sex partner. I'm very feminine and normal in this area. This part of a marriage is very valuable to me and I would be less than honest with you if I didn't tell you so. I don't expect any outstanding performances, and certainly nothing weird. The important thing to me is a good attitude in wanting to keep his woman satisfied and happy.

If you were married to me and you wanted children this would be OK with me. On the other hand, if you didn't want children this would be OK too. I could be happy with you either way.

If you're interested and are unmarried and truly unattached (not still in love with another woman), then I would like to hear from you soon. I would appreciate receiving a recent photo from you. I will answer without delay. Please tell me about anything you have strong feelings about, and any activities which you are deeply involved in. This would help me determine if I feel I could adjust to your lifestyle in a close relationship (marriage).

If you're interested in what I have to offer as a wife, lover, provider and lifetime companion, I would like for us to get together soon and spend some time together to check things out for compatibility, and determine if we feel we could develop a deep love for each other. If this resulted in working things out to the mutual satisfaction of both of us I would favor getting married without a lot of additional delay. The distance that separates us makes it impractical for us to conduct a long courtship with a lot of long trips and dates. The conventional courtship is out of the question.

If we did get married it would be necessary for you to relocate to Houston. My wanting you to do the relocating is not

How to Meet Men Using Personal Ads

a selfish motive on my part. The fact is it would be extremely difficult for me to relocate my business operations and ever get them reestablished and profitable. So, if you're tired of and disappointed in what you've had up to now, and tired of working (maybe caught up in a "treadmill to nowhere" type of job), and are ready for a first class woman to come into your life and extend to you first class treatment, please write me without further delay. If you can recognize a sincere letter, then you know that this is the "real thing."

Affectionately,

HERE'S A SAMPLE FORM LETTER TO USE WHEN ANSWERING LOCAL ADS:

Hi!

I LOVE YOU DARLING! How often have you longed to hear these words? How often have you longed to hold in your arms a woman who is loving and affectionate - to be cuddled, caressed and kissed, warmly, sweetly, tenderly? Perhaps you are my sweetheart - who knows?

This letter is in response to your recent "personal" ad. A little bit about myself:

WHAT I LIKE TO DO: I love sad movies with happy endings and happy movies with no endings. Have been known to wander the beach late at night just to see the moonlight playing on the water...Addicted to the horse races in Louisiana, the French Quarter, and tubing down the Guadalupe River in New Braunfels drinking margaritas...My leisure activities include mountain-climbing, canoeing, fishing, camping, hiking, bowling, playing the organ and guitar, reading, and I love all sports...I love poetry, books, walks on the beach and cozy candlelight

FINDING MR. RIGHT

dinners (I'll do the cooking). I enjoy movies, love live comedy theatre, all kinds of music (I love to dance), the desert, the quietness of the mountains, the ocean, sunrises and sunsets, and dining out.

WHO I AM: I've never been a game player. I never want personal happiness at the expense of someone else. If we have a single date or a lifetime together, I will never lie to you, try to manipulate you or use you in any way. I am an incurable romantic who treasures, cherishes and appreciates sincerity, integrity, honesty and warmth. I enjoy picnics, laughing, talking, touching, affection and physical closeness. A good listener who enjoys mutual spoiling...I'm a person who feels a oneness with the earth, who is in tune with nature, who loves the outdoors, and all things bright and beautiful that the earth has to offer, including rainbows, waterfalls, bluebonnet fields, moon and stars, mountains, the ocean, and animals... Also, I have a very positive attitude and I'm a goal-oriented person. I know where I'm going in life and how to get there.

WHAT I AM LOOKING FOR: LET'S BECOME GOOD FRIENDS, then...HOPE FOR A VERY BEAUTIFUL RELATIONSHIP. I feel that before we can have a good relationship, we must put forth the energy and time it takes to first become good friends. Friendship is one of the most important building blocks of a good relationship. To me, friends are like flowers in the garden of life...I am looking for a special, loving relationship with a unique man who is affectionate, handsome, slender, with a nice physique, sincere, easygoing, with interests and characteristics similar to mine - someone who wants a meaningful, serious, long-term relationship - not just a few dates. Are you that special man?...I am interested in a man who needs love, tenderness, sympathetic understanding, to share a long-lasting relationship with a one-man woman.

So, if you're disappointed in what you've had up until now and ready for a first class lady to come into your life and extend to

How to Meet Men Using Personal Ads

you first class treatment, please write or call me at 484-2525 WITHOUT FURTHER DELAY. Contact me today. DO IT NOW!

Sincerely, ADDRESS:
Sheena St. John
11540 Gullwood
Houston, TX 77089

P.S. Professionally I am a writer, author, own my own publishing company, mail order entrepreneur, and professional astrologer.

If you will follow my instructions on how to meet men by correspondence, I guarantee that your mailbox will be filled with letters and photos from nice men.

A final word of advice. If you live in an apartment, list your address as a suite number rather than an apartment number. This creates the impression that you are well-to-do and live in a high-rise penthouse. Also, if you're concerned about proposing marriage in a letter, don't worry about it. This is just used to attract men and show them that you mean business. You're in no way obligated to marry them. Then again, you may meet the man of your dreams.

Magazines With Free Pen Pal Columns and Pen Pal Clubs

This is another way to meet men overseas. There's a lot men overseas wanting to come to the U.S. for a visit, to live, or to marry an American.

Magazines With Free Penpal Columns

SUGGESTIONS: Do not send your photo and do not write a long letter. Address your letter to the PEN PAL COLUMN c/o the magazine listed. Send you name, address, age, hobbies. Do not make your listing over 20 words long. Many of these take up to four months for your listing to appear in print. No sample

FINDING MR. RIGHT

copy is sent unless you enclose a U.S. dollar bill and request it. All these publications are sold on newsstands in the country listed:

KODANSHA - 21-12-2 Otawa, Bunkyoku, Tokyo, JAPAN.
FILMSKI SVET - Vlajkoviceva 8, Beograd, YUGOSLAVIA.
MIN VAROLD - Fack, Stockholm 6, SWEDEN.
WOMEN'S LIFE - Box 245, Bloemfontein, SOUTH AFRICA.
THE CITIZEN - Hatfield Road, Box 1160, Salisbury, RHODESIA
RADAR - Mioosiez Swiata, UL Smolna 40, Warsaw 43, POLAND.
VOVOLINIS - 5 Irrodon Atticon, Athens, GREECE.
JAPAN MAGAZINE - Box 121, Okayama, JAPAN.
FEMINA MAGAZINE - Tallgatan 10, Halsingborg, SWEDEN.
MUNDO HISPANICO - Todas Los Servicos, Estafeta, Apartado de Correos 245, Madrid, SPAIN.
KARIMJEE - Box 1388, Mombasa, KENYA.
MITT LIVIS NOVELL - Box 315, Bromma 3, SWEDEN.
VITEK - Lidicka 14, Ceske Budejovice, CZECKOSLOVAKIA.
TONARSKLUBBEN - Malmo-C, SWEDEN
LETTERS ABROAD - 209 East 56th St., NY, NY 10022
ETHIOPIAN MAGAZINE - Viale Ireghse Taitu 51 Asmaara, ETHIOPIA.
PETRYS - Box 8124, Johannesburg, SOUTH AFRICA.
JOE'S PENPAL SHEET - 11 dewey St., Hudson, MA 01749 (charge minimum 40 cents per word).
RHODESIAN VOICE - Glenville Dairy P.O., Bulewayo, RHODESIA.
THE CORRIERE - Rue de dRussie 4, Tunis, TUNISIA.
NORTHERN TIMES - Kroonstad OFS, SOUTH AFRICA.
TONAR - Tidningen VI, Stockholm 15, SWEDEN.
SKIB-O-HOI - Fredhois, Oslow, NORWAY.
NOUS LES GARCONS - 9 Rue Humblot, Paris 15, FRANCE.
MOVIE NEWS - Box 543, SINGAPORE.
KAMRATPOSTEN - Sveavagen 53, Stockholm, SWEDEN.
WORLD MAGAZINE - Benczur Utica 34, Budapest,

How to Meet Men Using Personal Ads

HUNGARY CINEMA - Box 1574, Johannesburg, SOUTH AFRICA.
RAVE - The Tower House, Southampton St., London WC2, ENGLAND.
HJEMMET - Sorkedalsvegen 10A, Oslo, NORWAY.
AMARA - Rua Caldas Junior 219, Porto Alegra, BRAZIL.
BREVVENER EXPRESSEN - Box 341, Stockholm, SWEDEN.
FAMILIEBLAD - Byggmestervej 2, Copenhagen, DENMARK.
NOTICIA - Coca-E-Cola, C.P. 6518, Luanda, ANGOLA.
SVENSKA JOURNALEM - Fack 577, Stockholm 1, SWEDEN.
STER - Box 83, Mobeni, Durban, SOUTH AFRICA.
FAIKINN VIKUBLAD - Ingolfstrati 9B, Reyjavik, ICELAND.
BRERKLUBB - Box 6095, Stockholm 6, SWEDEN.
KAY CHEE - Box 372, Macao, ASIA.

Correspondence Clubs

Send TWO IRC'S (International Reply Coupons) with each query (to FOREIGN countries ONLY; to USA, send a first class stamp). IRC'S are available from your local post office.

ACQUAI TANCE WORLDWIDE - Box 1202, Addis Araba, ETHIOPIA.
BRITISH CHRISTIAN PEN-PAL CLUB - 17 Heyburn Rd., Tirebrook, Liverpool 13, ENGLAND.
PEOPLE TO PEOPLE - 2401 Grand Ave., Kansas City, MO 64141 U.S.A.
WORLD RADIO LISTENERS CLUB - Ankalgi, Tal. Gokak, Dist. Belgranm, Mysore, INDIA.
DX FRIENDSHIP CLUB - 7904 Coquina Way, St. Petersburg Beach, FL 33706 U.S.A.

In conclusion, listed here are some organizations that help find pen pals for prisoners: PRISON PEN PALS- Box 1217, Cincinnati, OH 45202 Attn: Lou Torok, Director. Also, FIVE MAGAZINE - 1220 Harding St., Box 2257, Fort Worth, TX 76101.

FINDING MR. RIGHT

Magazines and Newspapers That Accept Personal Ads

State	Name	Comments
AL	Country Companions 556 Kumquat St. Fairhope, AL 36532	Regional ads
CA	Chico News & Review 120 W. 2nd St. Chico, CA 95926	Regional ads
	BAM 1756 1\2 Las Palmas Hollywood, CA 90028	Regional ads
	Los Angeles Magazine Classified Bazaar Box 49999 Los Angeles, CA 90049	Regional ads
	LA Weekly 5325 Sunset Blvd. Los Angeles, CA 90027	Regional ads
	Pacific Sun 21 Corte Madera Ave. Mill Valley, CA 94941	Regional ads
	BAM 5951 Canning St. Oakland, CA 94609	Regional ads
	Suttertown News 2791 24th St. Sacramento, CA 95818	Regional ads

How to Meet Men Using Personal Ads

State	Name	Comments
CA	San Francisco Magazine 973 Market St. San Francisco, CA 94103	Regional ads
	San Francisco Bay Guardian 2700 19th St. San Francisco, CA 94110	Regional ads
	Santa Barbara News & Review 735 State St. Santa Barbara, CA 93101	Regional ads
	Couples 3420 Ocean Park Blvd. #300 Santa Monica, CA 90405	National ads
CO	Beyond Monogamy Box 6877 Denver, CO 80206	National ads
	Westworld 1610 15th St. Denver, CO 80202	Regional ads
CT	Connecticut Magazine Box 907 Fairfield, CT 06430	Regional ads
	Hartford Advocate 30 Arbor St. Hartford, CT 06105	Regional ads
	New Haven Advocate 1184 Chapel St. New Haven, CT 06511	Regional ads

FINDING MR. RIGHT

State	Name	Comments
DC	City Paper 919 6th St. NW Washington, DC 20001	Regional ads
	New Republic Magazine 1220 19th St. NW Washington, DC 20036	National ads
	Washingtonian Magazine 1828 L St. NW Washington, DC 20036	Regional ads
FL	Miami Magazine Box 340008 Coral Gables, FL 33134	Regional ads
	East Coast Singles Box 83 Palm Beach, FL 33480	National ads
	Florida Singles Box 8383 Palm Beach, FL 33480	Regional ads
	Sunshine State Singles Magazine Box 880 Boynton Beach, FL 33435	Regional ads
	Tampa Bay Life 4382 Prado Tampa, FL 33679	Regional and National ads

How to Meet Men Using Personal Ads

State	Name	Comments
FL	Tampa Magazine 4100 W. Kennedy Tampa, FL 33679	Regional ads
GA	Atlanta Singles Box 80158 Atlanta, GA 30366	Regional ads
IL	The Weekly 17 E. University Champaign, IL 61820	Regional ads
	One Times One Box 1365 Evanston, IL 60204	Regional ads
	Illinois Times 610 S. 7th St. Box 3524 Springfield, IL 62708	Regional ads
IN	Indianapolis Magazine 363 N. Illinois Indianapolis, IN 46204	Regional ads
IA	Des Moines Register and Tribune 715 Locust St. Des Moines, IA 50304	Regional ads
ME	Maine Times 41 Main St. Topsham, ME 04086	Regional ads

FINDING MR. RIGHT

State	Name	Comments
MD	City Paper 2612 N. Charles St. Baltimore, MD 21218	Regional ads
MA	Boston Magazine 31 St. James Ave. Boston, MA 02116	New England Region
	Boston Phoenix 100 Massachusetts Ave. Boston, MA 02115	Regional ads
	East/West Journal 17 Station St. Box 1200 Brookline, MA 02147	National ads
	Harvard Magazine 7 Ware St. Cambridge, MA 02138	National ads
	Valley Advocate 50 Prospect Hatfield, MA 01038	Regional ads
	Worcester Magazine 22 Front St. Worcester, MA 01614	Regional ads
MI	Flint Voice 5005 Lapeer Burton, MI 48509	Regional ads

How to Meet Men Using Personal Ads

State	Name	Comments
MI	Monthly Detroit 1404 Commonwealth Bldg. Detroit, MI 48226	Regional ads
MN	Twin Cities Reader 100 N. 7th Minneapolis, MN 55403	Regional ads
MO	Riverfront Times 1917 Park Ave. St. Louis, MO 63104	Regional ads
	St. Louis Magazine 7110 Oakland St. Louis, MO 63117	Regional ads
NJ	Ascension From the Ashes 153 George St. Suite 1 New Brunswick, NJ 08901	National ads
	New Jersey Monthly 1101 State Rd. Bldg. 1 Princeton, NJ 08540	Regional ads
	Atlantic City Magazine 1637 Atlantic Ave. Atlantic City, NJ 08401	National ads
NY	Selling Post 45-38 Bell Blvd. Bayside, NY 11361	Regional ads
	Mensa Bulletin 1701 W. 3 St. Suite 1R Brooklyn, NY 11223	For Mensa Members

FINDING MR. RIGHT

State	Name	Comments
NY	Ithaca Times Box 27 Ithaca, NY 14850	Regional ads
	High Times 17 W. 60 St. NY, NY 10023	National ads
	Metropolitan Almanac 80 E. 11 St. NY, NY 10003	Regional ads
	New York Review of Books 250 W. 57th St. NY, NY 10019	National ads
	Our Town 1751 Second Ave. #202 NY, NY 10028	Regional ads
	Pillow Talk 215 Lexington Ave. NY, NY 10016	National ads
	Village Voice 842 Broadway NY, NY 10003	National ads
	City Newspaper 250 N. Goodman Rochester, NY 14607	Regional ads
	Syracuse New Times Box 9979 Syracuse, NY 13201	Regional ads

How to Meet Men Using Personal Ads

State	Name	Comments
NC	Mother Earth News Box 70 Hendersonville, NC 28791	National ads
OH	Cleveland Magazine 1621 Euclid Ave. Cleveland, OH 44115	Regional ads
	The Scene 1314 Huron Rd. Cleveland, OH 44115	Regional ads
	Living Single Magazine 40 S. 3rd St. Suite 331 Columbus, OH 43215	Ohio ads
OR	Willamette Valley Observer The Atrium Suite 216 99 W. 10th Eugene, OR 97401	Regional ads
	Solo 1832 N.E. Broadway Portland, OR 97232	Regional ads
	Williamette Week 320 S.W. Stark Portland, OR 97204	Regional ads
PA	Erie Magazine Box 7159 Erie, PA 16510	Regional ads

FINDING MR. RIGHT

State	Name	Comments
PA	Germantown Courier 311 E. Lancaster Ave. Philadelphia, PA 19003	Regional ads
	Philadelphia Magazine 1500 Walnut St. Philadelphia, PA 19102	Regional ads
TX	D. Magazine 1925 Jacinto Dallas, TX 75201	Regional ads
	Houston City 315 W. Alabama Houston, TX 77006	Regional ads
VT	Vanguard Press 87 College St. Box 928 Burlington, VT 05401	Regional ads
WA	The Weekly 1932 1st Ave. Suite 605 Seattle, WA 98101	Regional ads
WI	City Lights 302 E. Washington Ave. Madison, WI 53703	Regional ads
	Isthmus 636 W. Washington Madison, WI 53703	Regional ads

How to Meet Men Using Personal Ads

State	Name	Comments
WI	Single Life 3846 W. Winconsin Ave. Milwaukee, WI 53208	Wisconsin and Illinois
	The Progressive 409 E. Main St. Madison, WI 53703	National ads
CANADA	Saturday Night 70 Bond St. Suite 500 Toronto, Ontario CANADA M5B 2J3	Regional ads
	Toronto Life 59 Front St. E Toronto, Ontario CANADA M5E 1B2	Regional ads

This concludes the listing of magazines and newspapers that accepts personal ads. Now the rest is up to you. Run some personal ads and answer some ads. You sure will not regret it and you just may meet the "love of your life."

CHAPTER FIVE

Singles Vacations

These are specially designed vacations catering to singles. This includes cruises, land vacations, and resorts.

The most popular and the most fun are the singles cruises. There's plenty of "hot action" and shipboard romances are the rule. Everything is so conducive to romance. There's just so many planned activities where you are thrown together with lots of nice men. All You've got to do to meet a man on a cruise is to simply say, "Hi." That's what they're there for. To meet women.

As follows, I will be describing three very popular singles vacations:

Club Med
40 West 57th St.
New York, NY 10019
Phone: (212) 750-1670 or toll free 1-800-528-3100

Probably the most popular. Their resorts are worldwide

Singles Vacations

and the surroundings are very romantic. Plenty of attractive and unattached men.

Once you have prepaid your week or two at the village of your choice, there is nothing to worry about. It's possible to budget almost to the last dollar what your trip will cost before leaving home. The only additional charges to be paid at any village are drinks from the bar, optional excursions, and personal purchases. The only sports activities you pay a small fee for are golf, deep-sea fishing and horseback riding. Also, scuba diving, but only in the villages of Ixtapa, Mexico and The Corals, Israel. There is a charge for materials used in the arts and crafts workshops. Everything else is on the house. A most popular feature everybody seems to enjoy tipping is never permitted!

WHAT'S INCLUDED:

1. Roundtrip jet air transportation from Club Med gateway cities for Public Charter and Contract Bulk Fare programs.
2. Roundtrip transfers between the airport and the village for Public Charter programs, Contract Bulk Fare programs, and group departures.
3. Accommodations for 7 or 14 nights, according to the Club Med village, based on double occupancy. Those arriving alone will be matched with a congenial member of the same sex.
4. Three tasty meals a day, plus unlimited wine at lunch and dinner.
5. Sports activities and the use of Club facilities, with equipment and qualified group instruction. No charge for sailing, wind surfing, snorkeling, tennis, waterskiing, scuba diving (except in the villages of Ixtapa, Mexico and The Corals, Israel) archery, etc.
6. Extra features: all-day picnics, boat trips, recorded classical music, nightly live entertainment, folklore evenings, and a disco.
7. Taxes and gratuities.
8. Baggage handling for 2 pieces of luggage (not exceeding 44 lbs.).

FINDING MR. RIGHT

Location of resorts are as follows:

1. AFRICA: Agadir (Morocco), Almadies (Senegal), Assinie (Ivory Coast), D'Jerba La Douce (Tunisia), Marrakesh (Morocco), Excursions/Morocco, Hurgada (Egypt).
2. BAHAMAS: Eleuthera and Paradise Island.
3. EUROPE: Avoriaz (France), Chamonix (France), Corfu Ipsos (Greece), Don Miguel (Spain), Foca (Turkey), Helios Corfu (Greece), Pontresina (Switzerland), Porto Petro (Spain). The following are ski resorts: St. Moritz-Roi-Soleil (Switzerland), St. Moritz-Victoria (Switzerland), Tignes-Val Claret (France), Valbella (Switzerland), Val D'Isere (France), Roussalka (Bulgaria).
4. MEXICO: Cancun, Ixtapa, Guaymas, and Playa Blanca. Excursions/Archaeological Villas.
5. MIDDLE EAST: Arzivand Eilat (Israel), Manial Palace (Egypt). Excursions available.
6. POLYNESIA/IN THE PACIFIC: Bora Bora (Tahiti), Cherating (Malaysia), Moorea (Tahiti), New Caledonia.
7. SOUTH AMERICA: Itaparica (Brazil).
8. THE WEST INDIES: Buccaneer's Creek (Martinique), Caravelle (Guadeloupe), Fort Royal (Guadeloupe), Magic Isle (Haiti), Punta Cana (Dominican Republic).
9. U.S.A.: The ski resort, Copper Mountain (Colorado).
10. BERMUDA: St. George's Cove.

Gramercy's Singleworld
The Gramercy Travel System, Inc.
444 Madison Ave.
New York, NY 10022 Phone: (212) 753-7595

They are celebrating their 30th year. Experience is often the best teacher and Singleworld's years of successful experience have resulted in the very finest tour and cruise program specifically designed for the single and unattached person - the never-married, separated, divorced, widowed and those traveling alone. As a member of Singleworld, you travel with

Singles Vacations

your peers, meeting other single people who share your interests, excitement, fun and adventure. Since 1957, more than 150,000 single men and women have traveled Singleworld - many of them "repeat" travelers - and the reasons are quality, service, and value. Not merely catch-phrases, but a way of life.

MEMBERSHIP - Anyone who is single or traveling alone is eligible for membership. Gramercy's Singleworld cruises and tours are open to members only. The membership fee is $20 per year (non-refundable) from the time your reservation is made. Their Singleworld Newsletter announces new trips, discounts & travel information of particular interest to club members. Ask your travel agent to enroll you now and reserve your Singleworld vacation.

BEST OF BOTH WORLDS - Singleworld gives you the best of two worlds - your own group of single people plus the freedom to mix with other vacationers on ships, planes, some sightseeing tours, and in hotels. As you enlarge your horizons and enrich your life, you enjoy the excitement and glamour of foreign lands, exotic foods, and the best of evening activities with other single men and women. You'll never experience the boredom or loneliness of the traveler who's on his or her own. Your vacation will be an unforgettable time of fun and adventure. It's twice the fun when it's shared!

WHAT SINGLEWORLD IS NOT - Not a lonely hearts club. Not a matrimonial bureau. Not a tour with equal numbers of men and women. AGE GROUPS: Under 35 and all ages. There are certain cruise & tour departures that are designated for single people all ages or single people under 35 years of age. These categories are spelled out carefully on each itinerary page in their catalog. In certain cases where no age category is indicated, the cruise or tour encompasses all ages. Group sizes vary and cannot be guaranteed.

TOP TRAVEL VALUE FOR SINGLE PEOPLE - Because

FINDING MR. RIGHT

Singleworld schedules more than 500 cruises and tours a year, it is possible to make highly advantageous arrangements. These savings are passed on to you. Best of all, if you wish, you can avoid the extra expense of single room accommodations by sharing a room with another member.

WHY ARE SINGLE PEOPLE PARTICULARLY PLEASED WITH SINGLEWORLD? - Because you have the companionship of members who share your liking for merriment aboard ship or on tour - without the added expense usually associated with dating. And you can go off on your own when the mood strikes - you are not "locked in."

Singleworld Cruises

Many departures sell out. They urge you to place your reservations as early as possible so that they may offer you a wider selection of accommodations and reduce your chances of being disappointed.

On each sailing, Singleworld's cruise escort helps with your cruise details, makes introductions, hosts parties and adds the personal touch that you appreciate. Two special cocktail parties are arranged for you and your single companions. Other parties, too! Dining room reservations are at the preferred second sitting with other single men and women. Of course, you may join the shipboard activities planned...tournaments, parties, poolside and midnight buffets, gala dinners, dances, professional shows, movies and other festivities. Wonderful days and nights are shared with your Singleworld companions. An unforgettable vacation!

In addition to shore excursions offered by the ship, your escort will arrange optional tours and evening entertainment ashore exclusively for Singleworld members.

BEST OF BOTH WORLDS. Your cruise ship is not limited to just Singleworld. You are free to mix with hundreds of other passengers - couples and singles as well as your own congenial Singleworld group. You will enjoy the best of two worlds.

Singles Vacations

Cruise Vacations Available

1. 5,6,7 day Bermuda cruises from New York.
2. 7 day Bermuda/Nassau cruises from New York.
3. 7 day Caribbean cruises from Miami.
4. 7 day Alaska/Canada cruises from Vancouver.
5. 7 day Mexican/Caribbean cruises from Miami.
6. 7 day Caribbean cruises from San Juan.
7. 7 day Mexican cruises from Los Angeles, Miami, and New Orleans.
8. 7 day Canada cruise from New York.

Land Vacations Available

1. Hawaii, California, or Colorado.
2. Kenya, 15 days.
3. Alcapulco or Cartagena.
4. England, 16 days.
5. Europe Spree Tour, 11 days and five countries.
6. Europe Grand Tour, 23 days and nine countries.
7. Europe Leisurely, 15 days and four countries.
8. Scandinavia, 14 days.
9. Alpine Splendor, 16 days (Bavaria-Austria-Italian, Dolomites-Switzerland-Liechtenstein).
10. Portugal/Spain, 15 days.
11. Athens Plus Stella Solaris Cruise, two itineraries and 17 days.

In conclusion, write for further information and their latest brochure.

Windjammer Barefoot Cruises
Box 120
Miami Beach, FL 33119

Telephone: (305) 373-2090. For reservations call toll free: 1-800-327-2600 (Nationwide), 1-800-432-3364 (in Florida).

FINDING MR. RIGHT

They offer singles only cruises. Their ships are large sailing ships.

There's never a dull moment. That's because you're not merely a passenger, you're part of a small group of fun-loving men and women. (Instead of wandering around on a huge oceanliner, you'll get to know everyone on board). WINDJAMMIN is laid-back luxury. Intimate shipmates. Sumptuous native cuisine. Comfortable air-conditioned cabins. And all the swimming, snorkeling, sunning and sunsets you can handle. With great fishing, beachcombing and sightseeing to boot.

They will sail you safe and steady to unspoiled beaches, hidden inlets and sparkling waters that conventional cruise ships can't reach. So you'll get all the Caribbean few others see.

Just call or write for further information or brochures on their cruises.

SPECIAL NOTE: Seasickness is a rarity aboard large sailing schooners since the wind on the sails prevents a rolling motion.

CHAPTER SIX

How and Where to Meet Wealthy Men

First off, remember ladies, you don't have to be a "10." This chapter isn't about the numbers game, so I'm not going to waste your time telling you how to be what some narrow-minded men think you should look like in their eyes. What you have to offer a wealthy man is YOU along with your attributes and faults. Don't offer a phony coverup or pat conversation. For example, if a man says he likes a particular hobby, lifestyle or whatever and it goes against everything you've always believed, it would be deceptive for you to tell him it's always been your favorite too, just for the sake of appearing to be the one for him. This whole idea most often backfires along the way, leaving the man feeling betrayed and seriously jeopardizing your future credibility. When you meet these wealthy men, above all be yourself!

This is not to say you shouldn't make an effort to improve yourself. Wear appropriate clothing when you are out meeting these lucky fellows. Don't overdress, as you will stand out in a

FINDING MR. RIGHT

way that won't help your cause. If you are on the golf course, wear something cool, casual, not too tight or too short and for heaven forbid, no jeans! If you're asked to a formal dinner, if at all possible, find out what the other ladies are planning to wear. If necessary call the place where the dinner will be and ask the maitre d' what the ladies wear when they come to his dinners. Hold back the excessive use of makeup. You want to blend with the surroundings your wealthy date is bringing you into, you don't want to make him feel he has made a mistake and not ask you out again. If you're not certain what is proper etiquette, look around you and follow suit. If you're alone with the man and you're not certain what drink to order or you don't understand the menu, ask him to suggest something or to surprise you. Also, you could tell him that you don't understand the menu and ask him to suggest something. Tell him you don't drink much and what would he recommend.

One of the cardinal rules in your search for the wealthy man is to forget the bars. The person you're looking for isn't wasting time in them. You have to go where the rich and soon to be rich spend their time. If you like boating and water, many yacht clubs allow people to join on social status who don't even own boats. What better way to meet a man with a yacht than to be a member of his club and present at the various social functions the club provides. This allows you to mingle with a lot of wealthy men without having a large cash outlay yourself. If you're a horse lover, find an exclusive stable or riding club and join up. This doesn't mean you have to have a horse of your own to learn to ride.

If you can afford the membership dues in a country club or if you can afford to borrow the money to join up, do so. If you are an aspiring golfer, most areas have places you can even rent the clubs. On public courses without restrictions, make sure you're playing during the middle of the week whenever possible. It's a common joke your doctors and lawyers are on the course during this time. Usually they play the country clubs but they have been known to play on public courses. The private clubs often have "men only" during certain hours. Find out if

How and Where to Meet Wealthy Men

this includes the club house as well. If the restriction lifts at four or five in the afternoon, make it your business to be there. There will be dinner, drinks and lots of conversation among these gentlemen, shouldn't you be a part of it?

Remember, you won't get asked if you aren't there. Better supermarkets are excellent meeting places for the upwardly mobile, as are better department stores. You can be working there or shopping there, just as long as these eligible men see you. Some of the really large stores such as Bloomies in New York have entire departments devoted to party needs such as wine, cheese, crackers or hors d'oeuvres, etc. Want to meet a nice on-the-way up type of guy, he's here buying for a fun party. Your bar room types don't come here, they're too busy looking for an easy pick up, without having to spend any money or nurture a meaningful relationship. It's a sure bet if you're looking around this type of party center, conversation will develop if you let it or even better, start it.

In University towns, the libraries are excellent meeting places for soon to be lawyers and doctors and other assorted professional types. Ideally, you should be in the University library as opposed to the public one. This could necessitate enrolling in one course to get the card entitling you to use the library. Take something fun and easy.

There are loads of opportunities to meet eligible, wealthy men while working as dental assistants, receptionists to doctors and attorneys, businessmen and the like. The pay isn't always the highest but it affords you the opportunity to meet a lot of different people including doctors, dentists, etc. Salespersons in prestigious car dealerships like Mercedes, Cadillac, etc. meet a lot of well to do men looking for cars and maybe you. There's also the opportunity here to make a good living. Real estate is always a good avenue to follow in pursuit of a good career and chances to meet wealthy men. However, here it would be best to pursue commercial listings rather than residential, as the latter constitutes a lot of young couples looking for homes. The economy is currently not as generous to realtors as it once was but this too will pass. For the moment,

FINDING MR. RIGHT

get to night school and get that realtors license so you'll be ready to meet those businessmen looking for investments when that market starts to loosen up. A lot of areas require a realtors license to show apartments for large complexes, (the kind upwardly mobile young men rent). Airline stewardesses meet a great many wealthy and influential men enroute from one meeting to another. Airline ticket persons meet the same people but usually don't have the time to start a relationship because of the lines and the need to get these people out. A stewardess can get more exposure to the wealthy passenger and perhaps start a relationship that will continue after the plane has landed.

Top waitresses in better restaurants meet a lot of affluent types who would love to get married and take care of you in a style you'd love to get accustomed to. Men's hair stylists and manicurists in barber shops, styling salons and other types of men's beauty care centers will invariably meet the well-to-do men, as there are more of them coming in for these services than the poor downrodden types of men you'd more likely meet in the local bar, honkey tonk, or whatever the watering holes in your area are called. Another often overlooked area in which to meet men is where you work but exercise a little caution in this area. If you find a fellow and he's married, but you still think he's the one for you, make sure he can afford his wife and you. Chances are good you'll come out second best in this area. If he divorces her for you, will there be enough left after alimony for you? Depending on your secretarial skills, you may be able to work for corporate executives, thus meeting other corporate heads in the process. Why work at a dead end secretary job for a man eight steps down the ladder when you can work for the boss or better yet, chairman of the board. The basic idea behind meeting a wealthy man is to be where they are in one capacity or another. If they see you with a certain amount of frequency, things will take their natural course. You will never meet them at work if you work on an assembly line, in a womens' clothing store or womens' beauty salons or as a telephone operator. In short, you need exposure either at work or at one of the previously mentioned clubs, golf courses, etc. The more familiar you become to them as when you're seen in their office, club, hair salon, etc., day after day, the better. The most important single thing is for YOU to be seen by them. Familiarity breeds relationships! Good luck ladies.

CHAPTER SEVEN

How to Meet Male Flight Attendants

Handsome and sexy flight attendants. Go to the concourses of any of the world's airports and you can see them walking in the airport. These are men of mystery. They are like birds in never ending migration. They have an air of confidence about them and are extremely poised.

This is a very proud and select group of men. Afterall, they have been screened and selected from literally hundreds of applicants to represent their airlines in this highly competitive industry.

I couldn't think of a more worldly man than a flight attendant. Afterall, how many ordinary men do you know who may have just had breakfast in Boston and lunch in St. Louis and is about to eat chop suey in San Francisco's Chinatown?

There are more airliners in the sky than ever before in United States history and there's a good chance a gorgeous-looking guy will be on your flight.

Flight attendants are really ideal for a warm, mature, and

How to Meet Male Flight Attendants

completely sexual affair. Why? Well he's not around very much; he usually is intelligent and outgoing; he can shower you with exotic gifts from afar; and lastly he has friends that are flight attendants also.

Now, let's discuss how, when, and where to meet male flight attendants.

This may surprise you, but the best place to meet a flight attendant is not in the air, but on the ground. OK, am I telling you not to approach them in the air? No, but you will be much more successful on the ground and I will explain why and where to find them later.

Here's how to approach them in the air, if you want to give it a try: After you're in the air and things have calmed down and things are slow, ask the male flight attendant for some coffee. Try to establish some eye contact while he's taking your order and be sure and give him a warm and sexy smile. Literally try to melt him with your bedroom eyes and tell him, "You sure look great today." When he returns with your coffee say, "Being a flight attendant sure is a demanding job isn't it?" This sure could open up an avenue for some prolonged conversation. What you're trying to do is establish as much verbal contact as possible.

After you've finished your coffee, call him to pick up your cup. This is when you're going to "move in for the kill." Ask him, "Would it be possible to talk to you in private?" He will probably respond with, "About what?" Just say it's personal. Whether you get to talk to him in private or while in your seat, this is the approach to use: "I'm very attracted to you and I'd like to get to know you better. Can we have dinner or a couple of drinks together?" That's all there is to it and hopefully he will say "yes." If he doesn't you can't say you didn't try.

Also, if you don't get to speak to him in private and you have to speak to him from your seat and you're sensitive about other passengers listening in on your lines, just have him put his ear down to your mouth and whisper in his ear.

You might try this if you get turned down for dinner or drinks. When you're getting off the plane, be sure and say on

FINDING MR. RIGHT

your way out, "Are you sure you still don't want to have dinner or a couple of drinks?" You never know, he just might change his mind.

In conclusion to approaching male flight attendants in the air, be sure and do it at the beginning of the flight. Don't wait until mid-flight or at the end of the flight. The reason for this being, that he may be tired or fed up with difficult passengers. So strike early and get a jump on any possible competition.

Now, I will discuss the best place to meet flight attendants, and that's on the ground. Particularly in the bars of hotels that have regular limousine service to and from the local airport.

Where do flight attendants hang out between flights? It may surprise you but usually they stick around the hotels they stay in. You might think they would be out partying till the wee hours between flights. This is just not so and here are reasons for this.

Being a flight attendant is not all glamour. It's a hectic physical schedule and it takes its toll on the body. For example, a flight attendant typically works only a couple of weeks out of a month. He will spend up to six to eight days at a time flying here and there which includes within the United States or internationally. Then he will be off another six to eight days to recuperate his body from jet lag.

When he's working the stretch and he gets off work, he's usually tired and catches a limo for the hotel and then straight to the bar. This is where you want to be to approach him.

OK, now you're in the hotel bar and a couple of male flight attendants walk in. By the way, I might mention that flight attendants are usually paired together when staying in hotels. Take your pick of the one you want to approach and approach him. Keep in mind that they are there for a few quick drinks and then it's off to the sack for some shut eye and relaxation. He's also aware that some good sex would be conducive to total relaxation. This is where you come in, hopefully!

You've approached him and you open up with, "Hi my name is _____ Can I join you for some conversation?" In most

How to Meet Male Flight Attendants

cases he will say yes. Now you will follow up with your conversational skills. Follow my techniques described in my chapter on conversation. Be sure and don't come on with a lot of B.S. about yourself. Revolve the conversation around himself and his interests. Try to avoid talking about his job. This will probably turn him off because it may just seem like one big long drag for them. It certainly won't hurt to sympathize with his hectic schedule and duties such as cleaning up air sickness bag overfill.

You're hitting it off real well with this flight attendant now. Hopefully, if he is with another flight attendant, the other attendant will excuse himself to head for the room to get some sleep. Once he's out of sight say, "I have a nice warm bed, clean sheets, and a potent nightcap at my place. So why don't you stay over at my place tonight?"

Your own your way now to total heaven now, providing he accepts your invitation.

The next morning you'll probably be up early. Don't be surprised if he's a little grumpy and irritable when he gets up in the morning. His body and mind are just depleted from jet lag and being on his feet. Just be warm and affectionate towards him.

When you drop him off at the airport, be sure and give him your business card (if you have one) and your home phone number. This way the next time he is in town he can give you a call if he would like a nice warm bed for the night and some friendly sex.

One sad final thought. He may disappear out of your life for long periods of time. Just accept this because it's a fact of life. When you least expect it, he will call and say, "I'm in town on a layover and I'm just dying to see you!" What he probably really wants is some good food, conversation, and sex. So why not give it to him, even though it's most likely not going to lead to something serious.

CHAPTER EIGHT

Unique Ways to Meet Men

I'm going to describe some very unusual methods of meeting men that can work very successfully for you. To use these is going to take a little courage and a matter of daring to be a little different, but the results are well worth it.

Circular Method

This is what I refer to as the "Circular Method." It's a very unique way of advertising for romance and several nice and attractive men will contact you. What you will be doing is simply putting circulars on windshields of cars in nightclub and singles bars parking lots.

This is how to do it. Have 500 circulars printed at your local print shop. Here's a sample of what to say:

"Single bars are great if you want to stay single. I don't. And I want a man who doesn't either. So, if you'd like to meet and get together and you are disappointed in what you've had up

Unique Ways to Meet Men

until now and are ready for a first class woman to come into your life and extend to you first class treatment, just send a photo and short note to:"

The upper part of the circular contains a black and white photo of yourself. The printing is done in large letters so it would stand out and is done on pink paper. Another option would be to list your phone number. Also, you could use a post office box if you want complete privacy. Just use your own judgement.

If you don't want to do the distributing yourself, you might consider hiring someone to do it. This could be a friend, teenagers looking for some spending money, etc. Also, if you live in a large city, look in the yellow pages under distributing services. They might be able to help you.

The best time to do this is between 10 and 12 PM when the parking lots are full, preferably on the weekends or ladies night. What you might consider doing also is leaving some inside the club. Just talk to the manager and get his permission. They usually don't care. Just leave some near the entrance or where you pay to get in. This is what I did.

In conclusion, feel free to use the wording on the sample circular or make up your own. So why not be brave, daring, and different and give it a try. It sure works and what a thrill it will be having your mailbox stuffed with lovely letters from the opposite sex.

The Book Method

What I'm about to describe to you is the best way in the world to attract men to you in bars and nightclubs. It's guaranteed to work and never fails! Men will literally flock all over you. You're probably saying to yourself, "That's a bunch of bull."

Let me explain the method. What you're going to be doing is reading in bars and nightclubs. Sounds crazy doesn't it? Now just place yourself in a man's shoes and you see this woman reading a book in a bar. Your curiosity is going to be killing you and you've just got to find out what she's reading and why in a bar. Get the picture now?

This is a highly successful method of attracting attention from men. Some men will even leave their dates to talk to you. You'll have a big edge on the other women because you're doing something unusual and different.

What should I be reading you ask? Well I'd recommend self-improvement and get rich books. Here's a list of the books I highly recommend.

1. The Magic of Thinking Big by David J. Schwartz.
2. Think and Grow Rich by Napoleon Hill.
3. Smart Money Shortcuts to Becoming Rich by Tyler Hicks.
4. How to Win Friends and Influence People by Dale Carnegie.
5. Psycho-Cybernetics by Maxwell Maltz.
6. Success Through A Positive Mental Attitude by Napoleon Hill and W. Clement Stone.
7. Think Yourself Rich by Norvell.
8. Magnificent Obsession by Lloyd C. Douglas.
9. The Magic of Getting What You Want by David Schwartz.
10. TNT, The Power Within You by Claude M. Bristol.

When you're asked why you're reading, you can go into detail about you wanting to improve yourself and you wanting to become financially independent. You tell them you're reading these books to motivate you and improve your life.

OK, now what to do when a man approaches you.

Most likely he's going to say, "What are you reading?" or "Why are you reading in a bar?" Then you close your book and you say, "Why don't you sit down and let's talk about it." Explain why and then follow up on your conversational skills. After you've made contact and talked to him for awhile, invite him to dinner the following day.

If for some reason you get interrupted before you can ask him out, I would suggest saying, "Don, this is very interesting,

Unique Ways to Meet Men

please call me tomorrow and we will discuss this further." Then give him a business card or personal card with your phone number on it. As a suggestion, you can use a folded business card and on the inside it reads, "I like you very much and I want to see you again! Please call me!

In the beginning you may find it difficult concentrating on reading with all the noise and commotion. With practice you can learn to block out the background noise. You'll be interrupted frequently by people's curiosity but that's the main objective.

So why not give it a try. It works and it will be a lot of fun having men coming to you.

The Card Method

How many times have you been attracted to men, let's say in public places, a good-looking salesman, a good-looking man alone in a restaurant, a nice-looking man getting off an airplane alone, a gorgeous hunk standing in the checkout line?

Well I have come up with a get acquainted card for those occasions where you don't have much time or the place is not appropriate for getting acquainted. This card breaks the ice and works like a charm. I've used it and my female friends have used it very successfully to meet men.

Here's what it says and you just take this to your printer and have it printed on a business card and on the back have your name and phone number printed. It reads:

I've been carrying this card for a long time hoping to meet someone like you. Bars & pickup lines are just not my style, so I hope to meet you using this card. I'd really like to find out who you are and tell you exactly what it was about you that attracted me. My name & phone number are on the back of this card. The option of calling will be yours, but I'll really be sorry if you don't call. Let's spend some time together. Please call and let me know who you are.

CHAPTER NINE

How to Talk to a Man

Now I will teach you the art of conversation after you have made contact with a man. Let me tell you what not to do first. Don't make the mistake of coming on with a lot of B.S. about yourself. Don't try to make a big impression by bragging about yourself or your material possessions. The trick to the whole art of conversation is becoming interested in him rather than trying to get him interested in you.

People aren't interested in you. They are interested in themselves - morning, noon, and night. This is an important fact to remember. After all, why should he interested in you unless you are interested in him first.

It is very important that when you're talking to a man that you face him and look him squarely in the eyes. When talking or listening to him, don't look off to the side or at the ground. Maintain constant eye contact. This gives him a feeling that you care about what he has to say.

During your conversation encourage him to talk about himself, his career, and accomplishments in life. Find out the

How to Talk to a Man

things he's really into such as sports, hobbies, art, music, etc. and really zero in on these subjects. This will make him feel closer to you while he's pouring his heart out about his favorite subjects. Just concentrate on talking about himself and forget about yourself. While he's talking, acknowledge him with statements like, "Oh yea", "Is that so?", "Wow", "You're kidding." Also, while talking to him, wear a pleasant smile on your face.

To sum it up, the secret to getting a man to fall in love with you is to talk to a man about himself. Try it and see how he will rattle on and on talking about himself.

Now I will cover some more very important areas of conversation.

Try and spice up your conversation a little bit with things of a sexual nature. After all, most men are obsessed with sex. Don't be afraid to tell him has a nice buns. Men don't wear tight-fitting clothes just for the hell of it. They are doing it to turn some woman on. They want you to take them to bed. Also, don't be afraid to tell him that you would love to make love to him. This really turns them on. Of course, you're going to run into the type of man that finds sexy talk repulsive. Don't worry about it. You're not after the real goody-goody type anyway. You want a man with no mental hangups and a healthy sexual attitude.

Remember to be nice in your conversation. Don't say anything mean or try to cut him down. Nice girls will finish first when it comes to meeting men. Be warm, charming, and pleasant.

Also, all during your conversation, call him by his name as much as possible. His name is music to his ears and to him it's the sweetest and most important sound in any language. This will make him like you. Now, don't forget to say his name often!

Let me tell you about the aggressive conversational approach that doesn't work. Initially, after just meeting him, you ask him to go to bed with you. Coming on too strong after just meeting scares the hell out of some men, especially if he is the shy type.

Expecting sex immediately after just meeting puts unneccessay pressure on yourself. It pays in the long run not to rush or

FINDING MR. RIGHT

expect sex too quickly or easily.

Of course, there are men out there who will go to bed with you at the drop of a hat, but with the threat of aids and other diseases a lot of men are particular with who they go to bed with.

So take your time and offer sex with gentleness and quietness. Don't force or demand sex. Let it happen naturally, with the two of you exchanging willing bodies.

If possible, use your hands, and particularly the tips of your fingers, when talking to a man. The light touch of your fingertips transmits electrifying signals to the other person which will support your thought messages with physical touch.

When touching him while you're talking, be sure it's in a subtle way. Don't do it in a way that would indicate a sexual advance because it may work against you. Just do it casually, like a touch over his hand or on his knee. He will notice these little gestures and slight touches and this will make him feel closer to you.

Finally, your voice is very important when talking to a man. Don't talk in a boring monotone voice. Put emotional emphasis on each and every word you say. Be sure and speak up and don't mutter your words quietly.

CHAPTER TEN

Body Language

You can attract more men than you can handle just by simply using the art of body language.

How to Use Body Language to Attract Men

Step by step I will guide you in the usage of successful body language using the following methods:

1. Develop a graceful, arrogant sort of walk. A walk that is free and easy with fluid movements. This kind of walk transmits a sexual message which will turn a man's head.
2. When leaning against a wall or whatever, thrust your hips forward, with your legs apart. This position also transmits a sexual message.
3. While you are standing or especially when leaning and you are wearing pants or jeans, hook your thumbs in your belt just above your pockets and point your fingers down toward your crotch. Because of your fingers pointing toward your crotch

area, this sends out a sexual message to a man and you will be amazed at how many men pick up this signal.
4. Cross your legs to reveal part of your thigh if you're wearing a dress.
5. Stand with one hand on your hip.
6. When talking to a man, let your eyes linger on his eyes and drop your eyes down to his crotch. Also, while talking to him, wet your lips with your tongue. By using these two techniques, he usually will feel rather uneasy and excited, thus you will be in control.

In conclusion, try these methods of attracting attention from men and see if they work for you. They have worked successfully for a lot of women I know.

Remember, the more techniques you use to attract a man the more men you're going to be meeting and that's the name of the game.

How to Recognize Male Body Language That Says He's Available

The following are some body signals and bodily movements that indicate a man is available and is approachable:

1. A man sitting with his legs open.
2. He holds his stomach in and chest out.
3. A man with a sexy walk, with his hips moving to and fro like the waves of the ocean.
4. He uses strong and sexy-smelling cologne.
5. Standing with one hand on his hip with his hip thrust forward.
6. Standing with his head cocked slightly at an angle, one foot behind the other, hips slightly thrust forward.
7. A man sitting with his arms crossed can indicate that he is frustrated and not having a good time and would welcome you approaching him.

In conclusion, keep your eye open for all these body signals

Body Language

and movements. With practice you can recognize these easily and it will help you to determine which men are available.

By being able to determine that a man is available in advance, your success ratio in making contact with a man will improve and you will move right in for the kill when you see these signals.

How to Recognize Male Body Language That Means He's Interested In You

The Following body signals and bodily movements will indicate that a man is interested in you after meeting you:

1. Of course, if you do make eye contact and exchange smiles this usually means that he is interested in you.
2. He sits uncomfortably close to you.
3. His hand or thigh carelessly brushes up against your thigh.
4. A man exposes his wrist or palm to you.
5. While talking to you, he twiddles his hair, rearranges his clothes, or pushes his hair away from his face.
6. While talking to you he strokes his thigh, wrists, or palm.
7. While talking to you he blinks more than usual, fluttering his eyelashes.
8. While talking to you his eyes are brighter than normal. He maintains eye contact and his pupils get bigger.
9. He sits with his legs crossed and pointed towards you.
10. He sits in a very straight position, displaying poise and good posture.
11. While conversing with you he licks his lips.
12. Eyebrows raised and then lowered, then a smile, usually indicates interest.
13. In a crowd he speaks only to you and focuses all of his undivided attention on you.
14. He touches your arm, shoulder, thigh, or hand while talking to you.

In conclusion, look for all of these body signals and bodily movements. They sure can be very helpful in evaluating how he feels about you. If you see he's really interested in you, really turn on the charm and give it your best efforts to make a love connection.

How to Recognize Negative Male Body Language

As you probably know, when someone is sitting or standing with their arms crossed across their chest, it usually means a person does not want to be approached and probably doesn't care to listen to what you have to say. This is how most psychologist interpret the crossed arms.

Don't let this mislead you though. When you see a man with his arms crossed he just may be frustrated and lonely and just not having a good time. However, if he has a stiff and tense look on his face and he is sitting in a stiff manner with his legs tightly crossed and purposely averts his eye when you try to catch them with your own eyes, you're probably better off not even trying to meet this guy.

A limp or hanging hand usually means he is bored, restless, or just tired. It can also indicate frustration or disgust.

For various reasons, some men do not want to be noticed. They may feel unattractive or even ugly or may not be dressed properly, lack self-confidence, and may feel inferior. They will just stand around shyly or bashfully on the sidelines staring at the ground or watching everyone else have fun. These men may have such a bad complex that they purposely do whatever they can to make themselves less noticeable, such as dressing plainly, unshaven, and wearing a non-becoming hairstyle. In essence these men are saying, "Just leave me alone, find someone else to talk to."

The really sad part about men like this is that some of them are really attractive. They just have a complex they can't get rid of. If you want to invest a little time you could help them get over this complex. It might be worth the effort.

CHAPTER ELEVEN

Looks

Do you need to be blonde, tan, and beautiful to attract and meet men? No. As a matter of fact, a lot of men are intimidated by beautiful women. Also, a lot of men are afraid to approach beautiful women. They take the attitude that they can have any man they want, thus they aren't worth pursuing. As long as you dress well, are well-groomed and have a personality and warmth of character, you'll get along just fine.

Some men even prefer a woman who is not very attractive, as they usually have a better personality and are more interesting. Just like a lot of handsome men, a real good-looking woman may just sit back passively depending on her looks and are so hung up on themselves they haven't even developed a personality. They're just plain boring and unexciting.

If you do happen to be very attractive, it will be to your advantage though. Good looks and a nice figure do attract a man's attention. Just remember that a lot of men are very interested in your inner beauty and personality. Looks aren't everything!

FINDING MR. RIGHT

Your hair is very important to your looks. Most men like a woman with long hair. Certain women do look very good with short hair but most men have always been attracted to long hair on a woman. Seek professional help to determine which hairstyle is becoming to you. Try a perm if you like. It can attract men like crazy, especially if it's thick and full. So, be daring and get a permanent and see if you don't get more looks from men. My single sister has been getting permanents for three years now and always get's compliments from men on her hair.

A word about jewelry. Jewelry is in, so do wear attractive jewelry to make yourself more becoming and feminine. Lots of gold really looks nice. Don't overdo it though.

If you really want to turn a man off, go out in public with your hair uncombed, stringy, and dirty, and wearing wrinkled, dirty clothes. Some women just don't take enough pride in their appearance and think they can meet men looking like a bum. Well it just doesn't work that way because a man likes a woman to be well-groomed. In public is certainly no place for a shoddy-looking woman.

If you happen to be obese, resolve here and now that you're going to get rid of all those ugly pounds. With the proper diet and exercise, you can trim yourself down to where you won't be embarrassingly fat.

It's a known fact that if you're a fat slob, your chances of meeting men are pretty slim. Obesity turns most men off. Unless you have a glandular disorder, this also indicates that you don't take much pride in your appearance.

This doesn't have anything to do with looks but it's worth mentioning. Be sure to take a shower or bath regularly. I've heard some men complain of women who approach them that smell like they haven't bathed in a week and what man wants to be around a woman that smells like a camel. This is a rare occurrence though because most women bathe regularly.

Last, and this is very important. DON'T LOOK DRUNK! Nothing is more repulsive to a man than a stumbling drunk asking him to dance or trying to put the make on him.

CHAPTER TWELVE

For Shy Women Only

What is shyness? Webster's defines shyness as being "uncomfortable in the presence of others." For the shy woman this refers to being uncomfortable in the presence of the opposite sex.

Shyness can be a crippling mental handicap and it's consequences can be devastating in the following ways:

1. Shyness breeds negative feelings like anxiety, depression, and loneliness.
2. It encourages you to think too much about yourself and to be over-preoccupied with your own reactions.
3. It will limit you in voicing your own opinions and values and speaking up for yourself.
4. Shyness hinders your thinking and ability to communicate effectively.
5. It has an unfavorable bearing on how others will evaluate your personality.
6. Shyness makes it more difficult for you to meet new people,

make friends, or enjoy potentially good times. Thank goodness, shyness can be cured and overcome!

As an example of shyness, at every nightclub you will find the shy woman. You'll see her just standing around all night, being afraid to approach a man and start up a conversation or even to ask a man to dance. So what happens? They get frustrated and leave the club. They keep coming to the nightclubs and repeat the same routine. They stand around wishing they could meet someone, get frustrated, and then go home frustrated and depressed.

You can overcome your shyness and you "must" if you're going to nightclubs. This kind of social setting can be most threatening and anxiety-provoking if you are a shy woman. This kind of setting will only aggravate your shyness condition if you don't take the appropriate steps to overcome your shyness.

In order for you to promote this change yourself, first you must believe that change is possible. You must really want to overcome your shyness condition. Last, you must be willing to commit time and energy to take action and to risk some temporary failures in initiating change procedures that can lead to long-term success. To sum it up you can change if you believe you can but it takes work...hard work.

Misconceived Beliefs of Shy Women

If I Ask a Man to Dance and He Turns Me Down or If I Talk to a Man and He Ignores Me, It's Because I'm Not Worthwhile or Good Enough For Him.

This irrational belief causes shy women to fear approaching a man and produces low self-esteem when they are rejected. This fear of being rejected and turned down prevents shy women from making contact with men.

If you're turned down for a dance, it doesn't mean that you're not worthwhile or not good enough for him. He just may not feel like dancing at the moment. He may just be tired. He may not even dance. There can be a number of reasons. So don't

For Shy Women Only

take it personally. However, what to do in a case like this is to ask him, "Would you like to dance later?" If he says yes, just ask him again later. In the mean time just ask other men to dance. Also, I might add, women do get turned down to dance, so don't feel that you're the only woman in the world that happen to. It happens to all women, even beautiful women.

If you approach a man and try to start up a conversation and he ignores you, don't take that personally either. He just may not feel like talking or being bothered. Perhaps he's tied down to a girlfriend or even married. Also, you just might not be using the proper social skills. So if he ignores you, move on to the next man and you'll find someone who will respond to your advances.

The Odds Are Slim of a Man Being Interested and Attracted to Me

This is the woman that has fixed opinions about herself and makes up excuses such as, "I'm not very lucky with men" or "I just don't stand a chance of meeting a man" or "There aren't any good places where I can meet a good man." These are just defensive statements to avoid placing the blame where it really belongs and that's on yourself. You just haven't tried hard enough to meet a man. That's where the real problem lies.

Make it a point to block these beliefs out of your mind because they will hinder you from seeking out men using your own initiative.

If I Stand Around Long Enough Maybe Something Will Happen

Nothing could be farther from the truth. Waiting around for something to happen will most likely accomplish nothing. This will produce little action, if any at all. I just can't tell you how many night's I've wasted at nightclubs waiting for something to happen, that is until I wised up. If you wait for a man to approach you and strike up a conversation, sometimes

FINDING MR. RIGHT

you will be waiting all night. You have got to take the initiative and create your own action, it's not going to come to you out of the clear blue sky.

Most Women Are Lucky That Meet And Attract Men

This is a misconceived notion that meeting men happens to other women because of luck and good breaks. Picking up or meeting a man rarely happens by accident. Somebody has got to take that first step to initiate contact with a man. The only difference between you and the other woman is she takes action, not because of a stroke of luck. So remember, you must go out and initiate action. You must make the effort to meet men.

If a Man Doesn't Show He Likes Me Right Away, He Really Doesn't Like Me and Will Never Like Me

This is an unproductive belief that a man, upon first meeting him, must show complete interest in you by verbal and non-verbal communication.

This is a perfect example of this misconception. You ask a man to dance and he readily accepts. After the dance is over he accepts another womans invitation to dance. You get all upset and you say to yourself, "If he was really interested in me, he would have found some excuse not to dance with that girl when she asked him."

What this girl doesn't know is that in the majority of cases like this, is that when interest is not immediately shown to the other, this doesn't mean that the possibility of liking you may not be there.

So, don't give up on a man if he accepts another girls invitation to dance. Just keep on pursuing him.

In conclusion, a lot of times a man will not show his interest in you following a brief initial meeting. Prolonged communication and conversation are necessary before he can feel comfortable in showing his interest in you.

For Shy Women Only

If You're Really Going to Make It With a Man, You'll Both Know It When You Meet and There Won't Be Any Problems

This is the woman who is waiting for "love at first sight" to occur to initiate a relationship. Upon meeting a man, if there are no vibrations or chemistry between them she simply dismisses the encounter. She uses this as a defensive excuse for initiating any intimate contact with men.

Waiting for "love at first sight" will prevent you from establishing real friendships with the opposite sex out of casual acquaintances. You don't have to be madly in love with a man to show interest and to establish a friendly rapport.

How to Overcome Shyness at Nightclubs

The following is a guide to use in overcoming your shyness at nightclubs. Follow these steps and you can overcome your shyness and start meeting men instead of standing on the sidelines watching other women meet men at nightclubs.

1. One the biggest roadblocks to a shy woman meeting men is fear. Fear that she will be rejected, fear that she won't know what to say, and fear that she won't know how to act.

Believe me, there is nothing to fear but fear itself. Fear and anxiety will produce distinct psychological consequences and if there's anything that's going to hinder your success in meeting men, it is going to be fear.

The fear of being rejected by a man can paralyze your attempts to meet men. Accept the fact that you're going to get rejected some of the time. Just because you get rejected by a man it does not make you worthless. There can be many different reasons why a man may not be interested in you at a given moment. Most of these reasons have little or nothing to do with you as a person. Being rejected by a man is just a risk you will have to take and if you do get rejected by a man, it's certainly not the end of the world.

Keep this in mind if you get rejected by a man at a nightclub.

FINDING MR. RIGHT

No matter how many men are not interested in you, you must remember there are many other men at the nightclub, many of whom would be delighted to know you.

To overcome these fears and meet men, you have got to approach it like you would if you were going to jump in a cold ocean to go swimming. Hurl yourself into it. TAKE ACTION! This is a real good cure!

You have got to practice at meeting men. Sure, you'll get rejected a few times. We all do. So what if you get rejected. You may never see him again anyway. By practicing, you'll build up your confidence. Also, by accepting the fact that you're only practicing meeting men, the pressure to succeed won't be so great.

2. Has this ever happen to you? You see this handsome man that you would love to approach. You try to build up your nerve but you make excuses like, "I'm to scared" or "I'm too nervous."

Pondering, stalling, postponing, reconsidering, these are all delaying tactics that impede action. If you find yourself telling yourself these lies and making excuses, block them out of your mind immediately and take action and approach that man right then and there. Don't waste any time or you'll see one man after another walk right out of your life. Don't delay trying to meet a man or you might find yourself delaying all your life.

3. Get rid of the idea that people are always watching you, sizing you up and evaluating you. The only people that do this are shy people who spend a lot of time fearing that they are being evaluated negatively. The reason you think you are being watched is because you do this to others.

The solution to breaking this habit is to stop judging and sizing people up and you will stop thinking that others are doing the same to you. Don't worry about people evaluating you unfavorably because the reason for this is that they think they are better than you.

4. Shy women have difficulty in carrying on a conversation with the opposite sex. You're going to have to work on sharpening up your conversational skills. If you don't have any skills, you're going to have to develop some. You're not going

to meet many men at nightclubs unless you talk to them.
   I have given you conversational guidelines to use in Chapter Nine on conversation. Put into practice these guidelines and I promise you that you will develop conversational skills and know how to carry on a conversation with a man.
5. Employ the methods used in Chapter Fourteen on "Meeting Men Using A Hypnotic Sleep Tape." Using these methods will condition your subconscious mind to meet men. Your mind will literally be saturated with meeting and attracting men. This in turn, will help you to overcome your shyness.
6. Use the "mirror technique" described in Chapter Fourteen. The only modification you will need to make on this is what you say in front of the mirror. Tell yourself these commands:

(a) "When I go to a nightclub, I will now feel very relaxed and comfortable around men."
(b) "I now overcome my shyness and meet lots of men at nightclubs."
(c) "When I see a man I'd like to meet, I now approach him immediately instead of making up excuses as to why I shouldn't approach him."
(d) "Now I'm not standing around all night waiting for something to happen. Now I make something happen. I take action."
(e) "Now I don't stand around waiting for a man to approach me. I'm now taking the initiative to make contact."
(f) "If a man rejects me, now I don't let it hurt my feelings."

   You can use any or all these positive suggestions or even make up your own.
7. Use the method outlined in Chapter Fourteen on "Meeting Men Using Mental Pictures." On your cards write the word "Confident." When you see this word, picture yourself at nightclubs as a confident woman in control, making contact with men. Picture yourself not being shy with men anymore, But a woman that is confident in her abilities to attract men.
   Another good word to use is "Contact." When you look at this word, picture yourself making verbal contact with men at

nightclubs. Picture yourself approaching men and talking to them.

8. Use the method outlined in Chapter Fourteen on "Meeting Men Using Autosuggestion." You can use the suggestions given in (6) of this section for your suggestions used for this method.

9. I highly recommend that you read books on shyness. There are many excellent books on the market to help you overcome shyness. In some cities there are shyness clinics you can attend which can be helpful.

10. You can order the shyness tape from POTENTIALS UNLIMITED. By listening to the tape daily for at least 30 days, you will become more confident and will feel an increase of self-esteem. Your fears and shyness will gradually disappear, in most cases.

To order this tape, write POTENTIALS UNLIMITED and ask for their tape catalog. Order the tape on shyness. The address is listed in Chapter Fourteen.

11. Finally, these steps to overcoming shyness can only help you if you have make the decision to change your life. The most powerful ingredient you possess in overcoming your shyness is the power of your own mind.

The key to making this change in your life is to believe that change is possible. Also, you must really want to change. You must have the willpower to commit time, effort, and energy to overcoming your shyness and to risk some short-term failures.

Overcoming Shyness Using Subliminal Tapes

I would like to announce an exciting and truly remarkable breakthrough in overcoming shyness with the opposite sex.

Even though I have written this book about everything you need to know on how to meet men, I too have had problems with shyness...I totally cured my shyness, using subliminal tapes.

While watching cable TV and flipping thru the channels, I came across a program about using subliminal tapes for self-improvement. I was really impressed with all of the inter-

For Shy Women Only

esting concepts and theories of subliminal tapes. Also, I saw many testimonials of people who's lives were changed after using these tapes.

So, I order the tape called, "Gaining Confidence With the Opposite Sex." After using this tape everyday for thirty days my shyness completely disappeared. I was very comfortable and confident around women. Take it from me...these tapes really WORK!

Before I go into what and how subliminal tapes work, here's how you can order your tape. Ask for the tape titled, "Gaining Confidence With the Opposite Sex." I might add, that this tape has a money-back guarantee.

Send $35 to:
The Joe Land Company, Inc.
Box 11156
Albuquerque, NM 87192
1-800-533-LAND for credit card orders

The Subliminal Reprogramming Story

Subliminal (subconscious level) audio programming tapes provide a dramatic means of removing the self-imposed limitations that keep all of us from reaching our full potential in any area of life that calls for attitude, confidence and performance. This relatively new concept "reprograms" the subconscious mind with millions of positive affirmations or suggestions.

The subconscious mind serves as our personal computer. It acts as data storage, retrieval system, and memory bank which takes in and permanently stores everything we experience. Unfortunately for most of us, the majority of the information stored in our subconscious mind amounts to negative programming or conditioning. Between seventy and eighty percent of the information we've received during our life is negative. Researchers estimate that the average child in America receives twenty negative messages from his parents for each positive, reassuring one.

FINDING MR. RIGHT

Popular self-help programs are often ineffective in bringing about behavioral changes because of this negative programming. If your "data bank" has inadvertently been programmed with suggestions damaging to your self-esteem, for instance, it's likely that you've continually found yourself failing in many endeavors ranging from losing weight to being financially successful. This is mainly because the information contained in your subconscious mind robs you of the self-confidence, creativity, imagination and even the desire to tackle projects which others may find easy to accomplish.

The word "subliminal" means stimulus, which is perceived and understood by the SUBCONSCIOUS mind without the person being consciously aware of its presence. SCWL subliminal reprogramming tapes by the Joe Land Company contain thousands of positive, reassuring affirmations covered with the sound of ocean waves. The listener is only aware of the sound waves, but the subconscious mind, being much more powerful and capable than the conscious mind, detects and understands the underlying subliminal messages. The effect of this direct communication with the subconscious mind is a gradual changing of the listener's attitude and even capabilities in the area being addressed by the subliminal messages.

Most experts on success, such as Napoleon Hill or Dr. Norman Vincent Peale, agree that "we become what we think about." The Bible even goes further telling us, "as a man thinketh in his heart, so is he." The subconscious mind works continually to accomplish what it perceives to be the goals set by the conscious mind. The subconscious, however, acts within the limitations or boundaries that have been imposed on it. Years hearing about the things you can't do and why "ordinary people" are doomed to live ordinary lives place severe limitations on your subconscious image of yourself and your abilities. Fear is the result of a perceived lack of ability or the belief that negative things will occur in our lives. Your subconscious mind tends to believe anything it's told. In order to develop the subconscious mind capabilities to overcome shyness, for instance, the subconscious mind must be repeatedly told, I

For Shy Women Only

AM confident, I AM comfortable around the opposite sex, etc. If these statements are heard and understood by the conscious mind, it simply doesn't believe them. Your conscious disbelief of the suggestions necessary to reprogram the subconscious will void the message and render it ineffective as new programming. If, however, the messages are transmitted to the subconscious mind subliminally, your conscious mind is totally unaware of what's being said and a totally effective reprogramming process begins.

There are several companies who now manufacture audio subliminal reprogramming tapes. While any subliminal message is effective in countering negative programming, the number of affirmations or suggestions contained on each one hour tape is the overriding factor in determining how effective the programming will be, as well as how quickly results are seen. Due to a secret engineering process known as the SCWL technique, the Joe Land programs contain between 80,000 and 110,000 affirmations per one hour tape. This is done using multi-tracks as well as multi-frequencies and tones. In special instances, a program can be produced with up to one million affirmations, but this process is still in the experimental stages and, at present, is expensive to produce.

Independent research studies clearly show that exposure to the powerful SCWL subliminal programming process is truly a life changing experience. No matter who you are or what task you've chosen to accomplish, you will feel yourself become a more powerful, confident, dynamic person as the reprogramming process continues.

How to Use the Joe Land Tapes

Using the SCWL subliminal programs is almost an effortless process. It is not necessary to LISTEN to the tapes, mere exposure to them is all that is necessary as the conscious mind is unable to perceive or understand what is being said. You will not really be CONSCIOUSLY participating in the programming process even if you tried to listen intentionally. Instead,

FINDING MR. RIGHT

you should implement an automatic process of as much exposure as possible to the sound of the ocean waves as you carry on your life in a normal fashion. You derive full and complete benefit from the programs by simply allowing them to play, at a volume which can be heard but is not distracting, during your normal, daily activities, such as working, talking, listening to music, watching television, etc.

The most critical factor is the amount of time the tape is allowed to perform the subconscious reprogramming process. It is recommended that a cassette player is purchased which has the AUTO REVERSE feature. These players, when set in the proper mode, will play the entire program continuously. When side A is completed, it will automatically play side B, then will revert back to and play side A again and will continue in this manner until the machine is turned off. They make this recommendation primarily because you will usually be unaware of the tape stopping if a standard AUTO STOP type of player is utilized. Using a player which does not have the auto reverse feature, will also provide a constant need to turn the tape over and re-engage the player. This will be bothersome and will detract from the amount of time the tapes are allowed to perform the programming process.

Ideal situations include the playing of the tapes at work during the day. This is especially effective for persons who perform their daily tasks in a relatively confined area such as an office or desk. These people should make it a habit to turn the machine on the first thing in the morning and then should "forget about it" and let it play all day. The volume should be sufficient to hear the ocean waves, but need not be loud enough to constitute a distraction for the user of any co-workers.

It is not recommended that the tapes be played in an automobile while the user is driving. While the programs will not be distracting, the sound of the ocean waves for some people, causes drowsiness. For this reason, users should examine the conscious effect the tapes have on them before considering use in their automobile.

For Shy Women Only

A number of people play the tapes at night while they're sleeping. There is no research to substantiate the theory that the subconscious mind receives outside stimulus or suggestions during the deepest stages of sleep. The subconscious, however, is extremely receptive to such stimulus during periods in which the user is going to sleep or is in the process of waking up. We, therefore, believe that there is at least one and one-half to two hours during the "sleeping" period at night when the tapes have a tremendous effectiveness. Playing the tapes during the entire nighttime period will have a positive effect; however, do not consider all of the time involved when determining how many hours of programming have been devoted to a particular subject.

Because the subconscious mind has the ability to perceive and retain millions of bits of information per second, the simultaneous use of more than one tape is highly effective. If, for instance, you wish to engage in the programming process using five different programs, you may listen to them all at one time by using five tape players. It is almost impossible to expose your subconscious mind to more stimulus than it's capable of understanding and retaining.

The amount of exposure time necessary for results vary from tape to tape and person to person. It is, however, recommended that exposure to twenty to twenty-five hours be allowed for each program before expecting measurable results. It is heartily recommended that the user play each of the programs being used at least an hour per day. Constant and diligent repetition is the most important aspect of program usage.

Many times a person will notice a major change in personality, preferences, characteristics or ability and fail to attribute the change to SCWL tape exposure. You should, therefore, be advised that the changes which will take place in your behavior will many times not "feel" as though something from the outside was responsible. Because the programs affect the innermost regions of the subconscious mind, the behavioral modifications seem to be a result of inner feelings and abilities. The weight control tape, for instance, contains affirmations

FINDING MR. RIGHT

dealing with self-image, self-confidence and other aspects of a well-rounded individual. In many cases, a person who has had constant exposure to the weight control program will find themselves with new abilities and confidence which have nothing to do with eating or weight loss. It is also important the SCWL user doesn't place limitations or time restraints on the expected results from the program. The subconscious acts as an enabling device, moving continually toward the accomplishment of what it perceives to be desired goals. If the user expects too little, or expects results too fast, the subconscious may decide that the job is completed prematurely or, in some instances, may stop working toward the desired goal because the time frame that is allowed is too short for its accomplishment. You should also "help" the process by consciously expecting a great deal of benefit from exposure to the programs while not limiting the period of time allowed for the desired results. In instances where the programs appear to be working slowly, or not at all, the user should remember that there are years of negative programming which must be overcome and in these instances, more time should be allowed and the programs should be played more often and for longer periods of time. As stated above, the ideal situation is for the user to play several tapes, simultaneously, throughout the entire day and evening.

There are for some people, periods of time that the improvement seems to have "leveled off," and they feel, even though they may have received tremendous benefit initially, that the programs are no longer effective for them. This is not the case and this person should continue exposure to the tapes until a "breakthrough" occurs and additional results are noticed. These situations occur for several reasons, the major one being a failure to notice subtle changes in seemingly unrelated behavior in an area which must occur before effects can be seen in the exact area of the program. In closing, try these tapes...they work!

CHAPTER THIRTEEN

How to Meet Men Using Astrology

A lot of men are interested in astrology or won't admit the fact and you can use this to your advantage. You can use this method very successfully in meeting men and getting a man to leave a nightclub with you to go over to your place and have his horoscope done. This can work for you and it's so very simple.

You may be saying to yourself, "I don't know anything about astrology." Well don't panic, because all you're going to need is one book to get you started. The book is called *Heaven Knows What* by Grant Lewi and is available at your local metaphysical or regular book store. They can order it for you if they don't have it. This book will enable you to cast a detailed horoscope in ten to fifteen minutes without the slightest study or knowledge of astrology beforehand. All you need to do is follow the simple directions carefully, step by step, and you just can't go wrong.

The chief use of the horoscope is it's aid in self-discovery or in discovering what makes your friends tick, not to mention the men you do a horoscope on. The horoscope tells

FINDING MR. RIGHT

the basic underlying psychological and emotional drives of the individual. If you desire to pursue astrology further after using this book, there are many excellent books on the market. I've been studying astrology for eighteen years and believe me, you can never learn enough about astrology. If you don't believe in astrology, investigate the subject and you will find there's a lot of truth to it.

Now, here's how this method is used to pick up and meet men in nightclubs. Of course, you can use this method in any setting or situation. The best time to use this method is after you have made initial contact with a man and towards the end of the evening. You can't just walk up to a man and ask him if he would like to have his horoscope done and then leave and go to your place. OK, let's say you have met a man and you have had a few drinks and a few dances and you're hitting it off pretty good. It's getting late and it's time to make a move. Ask him, "What sign are you?" Then follow up with, "Are you interested in astrology?" Then ask him, "Would you like to have your have your horoscope done?" Assuming he says yes, then follow up with, "Why don't we leave and go over to my place and I'll calculate your horoscope and let you read about yourself?" If he declines your offer for that particular night, set it up for another night. If you don't get him over to your place the first night, at least you'll get him over at a later date.

You have the option of making the main objective of getting a man to your place to have his horoscope done is to seduce him. After doing his horoscope you can proceed with your seduction routine (Dim lighting, soft music, a few drinks, kissing, stroking, etc.).

In conclusion, you're going to run into some men who don't want any part of astrology. You'll just have to try and convince them to try it before knocking it. If this fails, you'll just have to resort to other methods to get a man to your place. At least give it a try and see how it works for you. You have nothing to lose and a hell of a lot to gain. This method sure did work for me. Just buy the book and learn how to calculate a horoscope and you will be on your way to meeting more men.

CHAPTER FOURTEEN

Meeting Men Using the Powers of the Mind

The human mind is the most powerful thing on this earth and there is no limit as to what you can do and achieve with it. The methods we cover here will help you program your mind for meeting men.

How to Meet Men Using Self-Hypnosis

With the proper understanding and proper application of self-hypnosis, this method of meeting men can be highly successful.

First of all let me explain what self-hypnosis is and what it can for you. You must understand the relationship between the conscious and the subconscious mind. For the purpose of explanatory purposes consider the mind being made up of two parts, the conscious and the subconscious.

The conscious mind directs all reasoned action and the subconscious mind controls your automatic responses.

The conscious mind has been referred to as the "Mind of

FINDING MR. RIGHT

Man." With the reasoning power of the mind, women can direct her own destiny if she so desires.

The subconscious mind responds because of conditioned instincts. A good example is when you hear a sudden and loud noise and it makes you jump. This is not through reasoning of the conscious mind but from a conditioned fear in your subconscious mind.

The subconscious mind has no powers of reason, so every thing it accepts it is perceived as truth. It accepts and acts upon any fact or suggestion given to it by the conscious mind. While in a state of self-hypnosis you will practice meeting men successfully, even if you're a shy woman. All this will register in your subconscious mind and when it's time for action, your conscious mind will just simply act it out.

With repeated practice of meeting men in your mind while in a state of self-hypnosis, meeting men will become just automatic. You will feel relaxed and natural when around men and not feel nervous and tense when approaching them. Everything you do will have already been practiced over and over in your subconscious mind.

To avoid any confusion, let me explain that you will not be meeting men while in a hypnotic state. You will simply be in a light hypnotic state while in the privacy of your home while practicing self-hypnosis. During actual practice of meeting men you will only trigger your subconscious mind to act out the things that you have fed it to do. This is a natural process and as normal as walking. It's not harmful and every day you practice the use of the subconscious mind in your daily activities.

There are many good books on how and why self-hypnosis works, so I won't go into great detail on these areas. The main thing I want to do is teach you how to use self hypnosis to meet men anywhere.

How to Achieve a State of Self-Hypnosis

Now, we will learn how to achieve a state of self-hypnosis. First of all and most important of all, you must believe that self-

How to Meet Men Using the Powers of the Mind

hypnosis works, is safe, and have no fears about it.

Choose a room that is quiet and dimly lit. Make sure that you will be undisturbed because you need total quietness and concentration. You may choose to sit in a comfortable chair or lay in your bed. What I personally feel is more relaxing, is laying in the bed. The most effective method is inducing self-hypnosis upon retiring for the night.

Have no fears about inducing self-hypnosis because you're not going to do anything you don't want to do and you won't stay in a hypnotic state if you desire to come out of it.

The directions that you give to yourself don't have to be spoken out loud. You can give your commands silently in your mind.

The following is an example of a method to induce self-hypnosis:

Before retiring at night, turn the lights out and lay down in your bed and find a comfortable position. Close your eyes and repeat the following to yourself:

I am now going to relax every single muscle in my body, starting with from my toes to my head. Start with the right leg first, from the toes to the hip. My right toes are very relaxed...They feel very heavy and limp...This feeling is now spreading to my right ankle...Now my right foot is totally relaxed and limp...Repeat the same procedure for the left foot...Now both feet are totally relaxed...Heavy and limp...This feeling is now spreading to my right calf...My right leg is totally relaxed from my toes to my knee...This feeling is now spreading to my left calf and relaxing my left leg from the toes to the knee...Both my legs are totally relaxed and limp from the toes to the knee...This relaxed feeling is now spreading to my right thigh...Now my right leg is totally relaxed from the tip of my toes to my hip...Now I'm relaxing my left thigh too...So both my legs are relaxed and limp...Heavy and relaxed...So relaxed...So limp...Now I feel my right hand getting heavy...So relaxed and so limp...The fingers are getting heavy...Limp...So relaxed...My right hand is now totally relaxed and heavy...This relaxed feeling is now flowing up my right arm to my shoulder...Now I feel my left hand getting heavy...So relaxed and so limp...The fingers are getting heavy...Limp...So relaxed...My left hand is now totally relaxed and heavy...This relaxed feeling is now flowing up my left arm to my shoulder...Both of my arms and hands are now completely relaxed...So limp...So heavy...I am now going to relax my body...My hips...My back muscles...My stomach...My chest muscles...My shoulders...They will relax all at the same time...Now I will take a deep breath and hold it...I will release it very slowly...My entire body is now relaxing...I am taking a deep breath, slowly...My body is totally relaxed now...I feel so relaxed and limp...I am now breathing slowly and evenly...My neck is now feeling very relaxed and limp...My head is becoming so heavy...So very heavy...The muscles in my face are growing limp and relaxed...From my neck to the top of my head is completely relaxed...My body is totally relaxed...And so heavy...So relaxed...Every muscle and every nerve in my entire body is completely at ease.

The preceding procedure doesn't have to done word for word. The idea is to relax your body one part at a time until your entire body is relaxed.

After giving instructions to each part of your body to relax, be sure and pause until you feel it working. Be sure and don't will your body to relax. Your conscious mind comes into play when you will your body and this defeats your purpose.

When you have now reached the state of total relaxation over your entire body, open your eyes. Pick out an object above eye level. A good focal point would be where the wall joins the ceiling, a light reflection, a picture frame, etc. At this moment you will try to get your eyelids to close involuntarily on a specific count. You can use the count of three, ten, or whatever number you so desire. If upon completion of your count, you have an uncontrollable urge to close your eyes, you are in a state of self-hypnosis. This is the very first test in determining whether you have reached a state of self-hypnosis. When counting, go very slowly. If your eyes do not close upon completion of the count, start over again. They may close the first time you try it and then again it may take you anywhere from five to fifteen minutes. With practice every night, the time required for eye closure will decrease.

Let's say you attempt to get an eye closure but the test fails to work. The reasons you don't get an eye closure are usually the following:

1. You are not taking enough time to relax. Being in a totally relaxed state of mind is very critical.
2. You are not in a right psychological state of mind. Perhaps you are worried about something or your mind is cluttered with emotional turmoil.
3. Your conditioning process has not been sufficiently established.

If you are beset by any of these problems, just take more time to enter a good state of relaxation and tell yourself you are going to be in a very beneficial and pleasurable state of mind.

If all else fails, and this is very important, if you can't get eye closure voluntarily, then close them voluntarily and go ahead with the desired post hypnotic suggestions as though you were actually in the hypnotic state.

Here are some suggestions as to how to achieve the eye closure test:

When I complete the count of ten my eyelids will become very tired, heavy, and watery. Even before the count of ten is completed it may become necessary to close my eyelids. When I do, I will fall into a deep state of self-hypnosis. I will be totally conscious, be able to hear everything, and be able to give my subconscious mind suggestions. The following doesn't have to be repeated word for word, just the form is important.

One...My eyelids are becoming very heavy...Oh so very heavy...Two...My eyelids are growing very tired and weary...Oh so very tired and weary...Three...My eyelids are becoming very

FINDING MR. RIGHT

watery...Oh so watery...Oh so watery...Four...I can just barely keep my eyes open...Five...My eyes are beginning to close...Six...My eyelids are beginning to close more and more...Seven...My mind and body are completely relaxed and totally at ease...Eight...It is now becoming just impossible to keep my eyelids open...Nine...It is now impossible to keep my eyelids open...Ten...My eyes are now closed and I am in a state of self-hypnosis and I can give myself the post-hypnotic suggestions I desire.

Now using the following example, you will mentally picture yourself meeting men at nightclubs. Picture in your mind and tell yourself the following suggestions after you have reached a state of self-hypnosis and achieved eye-closure.

1. Before you leave, you look in the mirror and see a very beautiful, sexy, and charming woman. You have a very charming smile on your face and a sexy gleam in your eyes that can literally melt a man.
2. I'm going to meet a special man tonight and have the time of my life.
3. You walk in the nightclub and see all these handsome men just dying to meet you.
4. You start walking around to check out the action. As you're walking, several men notice you and your eyes meet.
5. You see an attractive man who catches your eye and you approach him.
6. You ask him to dance and while you're dancing you look into each others eyes and there's a powerful magnetic attraction between you.
7. You introduce yourself while dancing and ask what his name is.
8. When you're through dancing you ask him if you can join him for a drink. He says, "Yes."
9. You join him at his table or stand with him if he has no table.
10. You start conversing with him about himself and you start hitting it off real well together mentally.

How to Meet Men Using the Powers of the Mind

11. A slow song comes on and you ask him to dance.
12. While slow-dancing, you hold him close and your crotches are rubbing against each other. A heat of passion begins to build. He kisses you on the neck and then on the lips.
13. The song is over and the mission is accomplished. You have made initial physical contact and it will be smooth sailing the rest of the night.
14. Well, it's getting close to closing time and you ask him if he would like to come over to your place for a drink. He accepts your invitation.
15. After you get to your apartment, you fix him a drink, turn the lights down low, and put on some soft music.
16. You start kissing and caressing him and one thing leads to another and both of you end up in bed making mad passionate love to each other.

Finally, just let your imagination run wild and visualize anything you want happening to you at the nightclub. This is just an example. You can visualize yourself meeting men anywhere you choose after you've reached a state of self-hypnosis.

In conclusion, these suggestions should be carefully thought out and planned beforehand so you will know what to tell your subconscious mind.

Post Hypnotic Suggestions

After you have completed these suggestions for meeting men in your subconscious mind, give yourself post-hypnotic suggestions that the next time you induce self-hypnosis you will enter a deeper state more quickly. Using this technique, say to yourself:

The next time I practice self-hypnosis...I will fall into a deeper and more relaxed state of mind...Relaxing my body will come more quickly...And more easily...The next time I go to_____, my mind and body will be totally relaxed and self-confident...My mind will be at ease...The mental pictures and suggestions I have just experienced ...Will come into play...And meeting men will be as easy as pie...I know these positive suggestions and mental pictures will work for me...At the count of three...I will open my eyes...I will feel completely relaxed...At the count of count of three...I will feel totally refreshed...I will feel wide awake and alert...I will feel a renewed source of energy.

Alternate Method

The following is another method of achieving a state of self-hypnosis, along with suggestions for the subconscious mind.

Procedure #1

Choose a quiet room where you will be undisturbed. This room should be dimly lit, but enough light for you to read by. The room should have a peaceful and comfortable atmosphere.

Now, relax in your favorite easy-chair or lay down on your bed. Do not lay completely flat. Your body should be flat with your feet elevated, but your head and shoulders should be propped up with a pillow.

Get as comfortable as possible and close your eyes. Relax every muscle in you body.

Now clear your mind of all thoughts. Simply relax...and think of nothing. Think of absolutely nothing. Block out all noises and distractions. Keep your eyes closed.

Procedure #2

You will silently command each individual part of your body to relax (actually feel each body-part totally relax as you give each command).

1. Command your feet to relax (take your time and actually FEEL them relaxing).
2. Command your ankles to relax.

How to Meet Men Using the Powers of the Mind

3. Command your calves to relax (feel the muscles in your calves relaxing).
4. Command your knees to relax.
5. Command your thighs to relax (feel every muscle in your thighs relaxing).
NOTE: (Don't rush. Take your time between each and every command).
6. Command your stomach to relax (feel your stomach muscles relaxing).
7. Command your chest muscles to relax (feel them relaxing).
8. Command your shoulders to relax (feel them relaxing).
9. Command your upper arms to relax.
10. Command your elbows to relax.
11. Command your forearms to relax.
12. Command your wrists to relax.
13. Command your hands to relax (feel each finger and joint in your hands relaxing).
14. Command your lower back to relax.
15. Command your upper back to relax (feel all the muscles in your upper and lower back relaxing).
16. Command all the muscles in the back of your neck to relax (feel them relaxing).
17. Command the back of your head and scalp to relax.
18. Command all the muscles in your face to relax (feel your eyes, mouth, cheeks, etc. relaxing).
19. Command your entire body to relax (actually feel all your muscles, joints, nerves and mind totally relaxed).

At this point, your whole body should be completely relaxed. Your mind should also be relaxed and free of all thought. You should be thinking of nothing.

Procedure #3

Now you will relax your mind and body even more now.
With your eyes still closed...with your mind blank...and with every muscle in your body totally relaxed, begin to count

FINDING MR. RIGHT

from 1 to 20 slowly.

As you count, tell yourself that your mind and body are becoming more and more relaxed.

As you count 1-2-3-4, feel your mind and body becoming more relaxed.

As you count 5-6-7-8-9-10 etc., feel yourself going into a deeper and deeper state of relaxation.

As you count 17-18-19 and finally 20, tell yourself (and actually FEEL) that you are now in a very relaxed, almost sleep-like condition - with your mind and body totally relaxed and your mind completely free of all worry, problems, emotions, etc. Think of nothing!

You are now ready to give your subconscious mind suggestions. You must say these suggestions to yourself with "feeling" and "emotion." You must believe and have faith and confidence that these principles will work for you. This is very important to your success with self-hypnosis! You must "see", "feel", and "believe" each suggestion.

Putting Self-Hypnosis Into Action

After completing procedures 1, 2, and 3, open your eyes long enough to read the following suggestion. Read it to yourself a few times...

"I AM COMPLETELY RELAXED WHENEVER I SPEAK MEN"

Now...close your eyes and repeat the suggestion to yourself several more times...WITH BELIEF!

As you say the suggestion to yourself, SEE yourself talking to men. FEEL yourself being totally relaxed while talking to them. BELIEVE that you actually are completely relaxed as you talk to men.

How to Meet Men Using the Powers of the Mind

Procedure #4

Open your eyes just long enough to read the next suggestion. Read it a few times.

"I AM TOTALLY CONFIDENT AND COMPLETELY SELF-ASSURED WHENEVER I SPEAK TO MEN - ESPECIALLY HANDSOME MEN"

Now, close your eyes and repeat the above suggestion to yourself several more times. And...as before...repeat it to yourself with belief.
As you say the above suggestion to yourself, SEE yourself talking to men. SEE yourself talking to handsome men. BELIEVE that you actually do have a the confidence and self-assurance necessary to hold a conversation with absolutely any man you choose.

Procedure #5

Go through the remaining suggestions following the same procedure as outlined above.
NOTE: It is very, very important that you use the SEE...FEEL...BELIEVE technique for each suggestion. This is the only way you will be able to reach your subconscious mind, and thus, receive positive results.
NOTE: You are to open your eyes between each suggestion ONLY until they are memorized. Once memorized, simply keep your eyes closed throughout the entire procedure. You should memorize the suggestions as soon as possible...as it will be more beneficial to you to keep your eyes closed throughout the entire procedure.
NOTE: Do not get discouraged if you find it somewhat awkward (at first) when trying to "see", "feel", and "believe" each suggestion. This is to be expected.
You will become more and more at ease with these principles each day you practice them.

FINDING MR. RIGHT

Your Remaining Daily Suggestions

* I ALWAYS SAY THE RIGHT THINGS WHENEVER I SPEAK TO MEN. I ALWAYS KNOW EXACTLY WHAT TO SAY.
* I ALWAYS KNOW WHAT NOT TO SAY TO MEN.
* I NEVER HAVE TO ACT "COOL" WITH MEN. I AM COOL ENOUGH THE WAY I AM. MEN NOTICE THIS QUALITY IN ME AND LIKE ME FOR BEING MYSELF.
* IT IS EXTREMELY EASY FOR ME TO WALK UP TO ANY MAN AND START TALKING TO HIM.
* WHEN I SEE A MAN I LIKE, I AM ABLE TO MOVE INTO ACTION QUICKLY AND EASILY.
* I REALIZE THAT SOME MEN SIMPLY ARE NOT INTERESTED IN WOMEN...SO IF I GET TURNED DOWN BY A MAN, I QUICKLY FORGET ABOUT IT AND MOVE ON TO ANOTHER MAN.
* EACH TIME I TRY TO MEET A MAN IS EASIER THAN THE TIME BEFORE.
* WHENEVER I APPROACH A MAN, I AM TOTALLY FREE FROM ALL NEGATIVE FEELINGS...SUCH AS WORRY, INFERIORITY OR NERVOUSNESS.
* I ALWAYS THINK IN TERMS OF SUCCEEDING WHENEVER I APPROACH A MAN. I NEVER THINK IN TERMS OF FAILURE.
* I ALWAYS EXPECT MEN TO SAY "YES" WHENEVER I SUGGEST WE GET TOGETHER SOMETIME.
* I REALIZE THAT MOST MEN I MEET ARE QUIET ANXIOUS TO HAVE ME ASK THEM FOR A DATE. KNOWING THIS, I AM COMPLETELY RELAXED AND SELF-CONFIDENT WHENEVER I ASK A MAN FOR A DATE.
* KNOWING THAT IT IS NATURAL FOR A GIRL TO WAIT FOR THE MAN TO MAKE THE FIRST MOVE WHEN IT COMES TO SEX, I FOLLOW MY SEXUAL URGES AND PROCEED TO SEDUCE MY DATE WHENEVER I FEEL THE TIME IS RIGHT.

How to Meet Men Using the Powers of the Mind

* MY FAILURE DAYS WITH MEN ARE GONE FOREVER. I AM A NEW WOMAN AND SEE MYSELF THROUGH THE "SUCCESS" EYE OF NOW.
* I PUSH DEFEAT INTO MY PAST...AND LOOK BEYOND IT FOR SUCCESS.
* I CLOSE THE DOOR TIGHTLY ON MY PAST BAD EXPERIENCES WITH MEN...AND KEEP IT CLOSED.
* I AM A MATURE PERSON AND SEEK EVEN GREATER GROWTH WITHIN MYSELF.
* AS FAR AS MEETING, DATING, AND SEDUCING MEN IS CONCERNED, I HAVE ABSOLUTELY NO LIMITATIONS.
* I AM SUCCESSFUL IN ALL MY RELATIONS WITH MEN.

Procedure #6

After completing your daily suggestions, remain relaxed. Remain in the same position and relax your whole body. Think of nothing...keep your eyes closed...and just relax...Now just relax...relax...relax...relax and enjoy it...relax...

After two or three minutes of this you will be ready to come out of self-hypnosis.

Coming Out of Self-Hypnosis

With your eyes still closed...and your mind blank...start counting backwards from 20 down to 1. Count slowly.

As you count down...20-19-18-17-16-15...feel your body and mind begin to "awaken." (Your eyes should remain closed).

As you count down...14-13-12-11-10...start to become aware of the sounds and atmosphere around you.

As you count down...9-8-7-6...say to yourself: "When I open my eyes, I will feel simply GREAT! I will feel totally rested and greatly refreshed. When I open my eyes, I will feel great. I will be full of energy and will feel greatly refreshed." (All the while you are saying the above, believe it!).

As you count down...5-4-3-2..."feel" yourself starting to

FINDING MR. RIGHT

feel just great. "FEEL" yourself starting to come "alive."

And finally, as you say 1...OPEN YOUR EYES...and immediately GET UP!!!

FINAL NOTE: Each self-hypnosis session should last about twenty minutes. And you should have a session once a day...every day.

Also, do not use these principles very late at night or when you are very tired. By doing so, you may easily fall asleep (something which we do not want to happen).

The best time to practice self-hypnosis is midmorning, midafternoon, or evening.

Use either of these self-hypnosis methods or both. They are both equally effective. With practice, you will be amazed at the results. You will be meeting more men and doing it more easily. It will just come naturally to you.

How to Meet Men Using a Hypnotic Sleep Tape

Within you is the ability to pick up or meet any man you desire. It is only awaiting the stimulation of your desire to spring forth and bring you whatever man you want.

You have the key to that door. Only you can unlock it. ONLY YOU. And for you a hypnotic sleep tape can be the first step in unlocking that door.

Potentials Unlimited of Grand Rapids, Michigan offers a self-hypnosis tape containing complete instructions on how to give yourself suggestions, along with detailed procedures for entering a state of self-hypnosis.

Using it, you will be guided into a state of hypnosis with key phrases and statements so you can utilize this level of mind anytime you choose. When you have reached a good depth, there's a quiet space on the tape where you can enter your own suggestions into your subconscious mind. Then, after a bit, you're guided back to awakening consciousness.

At the end of this chapter I will tell you which suggestions to enter in the quiet space on the tape and how to order this tape.

How to Meet Men Using the Powers of the Mind

How Hypnotic Sleep Tapes Work

Each of these professionally produced tapes are designed to bypass your conscious mind. It is this, the subconscious, that is the real power center of your being. The subconscious mind is the seat of memory, the monitor of all bodily processes. It regulates your heart, plays chemist for your digestive system, and analyzes input from your senses like an ultra-sophisticated computer (which it is). Your subconscious is a magical property, existing deep within you.

Your subconscious will accept, then bring into reality, any suggestion presented to it. When the suggestions are positive, dominate, and accompanied with visual imagery, as in hypnosis, the results are amazing.

How Hypnotic Sleep Tapes Are Used at Bedtime

Using a hypnotic sleep cassette tape, a series of suggestions are first given to your conscious mind to bring about a pleasant state of relaxation.

If the tape is played at your sleep time, you will probably drift off into a natural sleep. This is highly desirable because the subconscious mind never sleeps, and will accept suggestions far better without my interference from your conscious mind.

Repeated playing of the tape at bedtime will completely saturate the subconscious mind with positive suggestions, designed to bring about positive changes within you.

How Hypnotic Sleep Tapes Are Used During the Day

Your conscious mind will not be fully aware of the suggestions given to your subconscious. Therefore, playing the tape several times a week in a relaxing and restful position will be necessary.

Listening to the tape during the day will allow you to experience the pleasant sensations of light hypnosis. You will find yourself floating smoothly into a dreamlike state of mind,

FINDING MR. RIGHT

much like twilight sleep or daydreaming.

During this daytime playing, your conscious mind will become saturated with the same messages your subconscious mind has been absorbing during the evening.

How It All Works Together For You

By using the tape at two different times, your conscious and subconscious mind will begin to work in harmony. The results are dramatic. Positive changes you've desired happen and you meet men as if by magic.

It's your mind and it's programming that makes up your world.

Look around at your world. What would you like to change, eliminate, to improve, to make better for yourself?

Hypnosis is a very effective tool for change. Hypnotic sleep tapes are simple, easy, inexpensive ways to achieve this change. In fact, they could be the most important thing you've ever done for your life, not to mention your love-life.

How to Use Your Sleep Tape to Meet Men

Write or call Potentials Unlimited and ask for their latest tape catalog at this address below:

POTENTIALS UNLIMITED
Box 891
GRAND RAPIDS, MI 49518
(616) 949-7894

Order the tape entitled, "SELF-HYPNOSIS CAN CHANGE YOUR LIFE." Using this tape you will be put into a state of self-hypnosis with key phrases and statements so you can put into use this level of mind anytime you desire. There's a quiet space on the tape where you can enter your own suggestions into your mind.

Now I will give you an example of the suggestions to use.

How to Meet Men Using the Powers of the Mind

You don't have to use these suggestions word for word. You can make up your own suggestions for any type of circumstance or situation for meeting men. Here's a sample recording:

As I'm getting ready to go to the nightclub tonight, I look into the mirror and see this beautiful and attractive woman, a woman with a very sexy look about her with a charming smile that can literally melt a man...Before I leave I'm thoroughly convinced in my mind that I will meet a special man at the nightclub...Upon arriving at the nightclub I will feel very confident and totally relaxed...As I walk thru the nightclub to check out the action, I catch the eyes of several attractive men...They're all giving me that, "I'd love to meet you" look...There's so many eligible men to choose from it's unbelievable...I can have any man I desire...While cruisin the nightclub I see this very attractive man and our eyes meet...The magnetism between us is overpowering...I approach him and say, "Hi, would you like to dance?"...He says, "Yes, I'd love to"...We get out on the dance floor and start dancing to the pulsating beat...Watching the way he moves his hips and crotch are driving me out of my mind...Our eyes meet and we both smile...I can tell by the way he looks at me that he's interested in me...I ask him, "What's your name?"...Then he tells me his name...The song ends and we're having such a good time we keep on dancing on and on...We mutually agree to take a break and I say, "Can I join you for some conversation?"...He replies, "Sure"...I join him at his table and begin getting him to talk about himself...By this time we're really hitting it off real good conversationally...After making this initial contact, I ask him to dance again...We dance several songs again and we both feel drawn to each other like magnets...Finally a slow song comes on...Now is my chance to make some real physical contact...Our bodies meet and I can feel my warm breasts against his chest...As we dance, our crotches begin to rub...I begin to caress his back with my hands and he does the same to me...I begin kissing his neck and working my way up to his ear lobe...He's becoming just as excited as I am and begins kissing me very gently and softly

FINDING MR. RIGHT

my neck...Now our lips meet and the vibrations are so strong we can hardly keep our balance while dancing...I'm having the time of my life tonight and I feel so good...The song ends and we return to our table...It's getting kind of late now...I ask him if he would like to leave and get something to eat...He accepts the invitation and we go to a restaurant...After we finish our food, I ask him if he would like to come over for a drink...He accepts and before you know it we are at my apartment...I fix him a drink and put some soft music on and turn the lights down low...We both are feeling so relaxed and comfortable...Our lips meet and the passion begins building up...He is responding to all my physical advances...I begin undressing him and then take off my clothes...Now we are making mad passionate love to each other...He spends the night and before he goes home I get his phone number for future reference...My head is up in the clouds and I keep saying to myself, "It's so easy meeting men at nightclubs"...I'm going back again and I will make a love connection again...This I'm sure of...And sure enough, I go back and the same things happen all over again...This is really exciting meeting so many different men and being so successful at it...I can attract any man I desire...I'm the envy of all the women that just stand around on the sidelines...They're amazed at my ability to meet men...I am totally confident in my abilities and skill in meeting men at nightclubs or anywhere.

Using this tape can do wonders for your lovelife. Just listen to it before you retire at night and once during the day while you are awake. You should listen to this tape for at least 30 days to get the full benefit from it.

How to Meet Men Using Autosuggestion

This will help you to meet men by influencing the subconscious mind by means of suggestion. Using the method of autosuggestion, you will be giving yourself positive suggestions to meet men.

This method is very simple and very effective. Repetition

How to Meet Men Using the Powers of the Mind

is the main rule in making suggestions work. They should be repeated three or four times, or even more. These suggestions can be made verbally, though it is not necessary to say the words aloud. Just thinking them is enough. Some people respond better if they are said aloud, so you might want to experiment to see what works best for you. To make the suggestion more potent, you may form a visual image while making the suggestion verbally. There is a tendency for the subconscious to carry out any prolonged and repeated visual image.

You will be phrasing your suggestions using the words, "I can" or "I will." Start out using the words, "I can" and if no results are shown, switch over to the words, "I will." Remember, in giving yourself suggestions, acceptance by the inner mind is necessary or it will not be carried out, no matter how badly you may consciously want this.

Now I will recommend these suggestions for you to use. Pick out the ones you like the most or even make up your own. Any of them will work.

"I can walk up to any man and start talking to him."
"I can move into action quickly and easily when I see a man I like."
"I can approach a man, totally free from all negative feelings such as worry, inferiority or nervousness."
"I can make the first move when it comes to sex and follow my sexual urges and proceed to seduce my date whenever I feel the time is right."
"I can bring a man home with me if I choose to do so, when I go to nightclubs."
"I can meet up any man I desire."

Also, you might want to try this while giving yourself suggestions. In the book, Self-Suggestion (Huna Research Publications - Vista, California), Max Long recommends the use of deep breathing while you give yourself suggestions. He recommends that you concentrate deeply on the suggestion while breathing deeply and hard. To employ this method, just concentrate for a moment on your suggestion, pause, start concentrating on your suggestion again, and continue to repeat this back and forth, all while breathing deeply.

It is recommended that you shouldn't burden your subconscious mind with too many suggestions at one time. Try to work on one suggestion at a time and never more than two. If using two suggestions, start with the first one and repeat it three or four times, then repeat the second suggestion three or four times, then go back and repeat the first suggestion.

Use this method daily and you will be meeting more men than you ever dreamed possible. You will be more confident than ever and meeting men will become natural and easy. Try this and see if your love-life doesn't improve dramatically.

Also, I might add, you can use this method to obtain anything you want. It doesn't have to be applied to just meeting men only.

In conclusion, remember the need for repetition and suggest results, not means.

The Mirror Technique For Meeting Men

This is a very effective method of releasing the power of the subconscious mind by using a mirror. This method is very effective in motivating you to meet men. It can be used to obtain anything you so desire.

Now I will explain the technique. Stand in front of a mirror. The mirror does not have to be full length, but you should at least be able to see yourself from the waste up.

Stand fully erect just like a soldier does when told to come to attention. Now take three or four deep breaths until you feel a sense of enormous strength, power, and determination. Now look into the very depths of your eyes and tell yourself, "Everytime I go to a nightclub I will meet a very special man that I'm attracted to." This is just an example of what to tell yourself and be sure to say this aloud so you can see your lips move and hear the words uttered. Also, you can make up your own words and suggestions or even use the ones in the previous section on

How to Meet Men Using the Powers of the Mind

autosuggestion.

Do this exercise regularly at least twice a day, in the morning and in the evening and you will be astonished at the results. You may augment this by writing any slogans or key words associated with your desires with soap on the face of your mirror, such as "LOVE CONNECTION", "TAKE ACTION", etc.

Within a few days after practicing this exercise you will really begin to feel a sense of confidence in yourself and your abilities to meet men that you never have felt before.

It is advisable not to tell anyone about your using this method to meet men. There are scoffers and skeptics that may ridicule you and shake your confidence and you certainly don't want your confidence shaken, particularly if you are just beginning to learn this science.

Meeting Men Using Mental Pictures

It is known fact that whatever a woman can conceive mentally, she can bring into materialization. Meeting men must follow if the proper mental pictures are created and maintained, for this sets in motion the law of cause and effect.

To help you create the mental pictures of meeting men, I will describe a very effective method to saturate your subconscious mind with mental pictures.

You will need about four cards. The back of business cards will do just great. Just write the word, "LOVE CONNECTION" or any other word you associate with meeting men with on these cards. Carry one in your purse, place one on your bathroom mirror, place one by your bed, then another one where you work. Whenever you look at these cards, mentally picture yourself meeting men at various places such as nightclubs, the beach, swimming pools, etc. By placing these cards in various areas, this will enable you to see mentally, the pictures at all hours of the day.

In addition to using the cards during the day, it is best to look at them before you go to sleep at night and upon awaking in the morning and mentally picture yourself meeting many men.

These two periods of the day are highly important moments to concentrate upon thoughts with added force. It is helpful to form these pictures throughout the day because the more often you form your pictures backed with desire, the speedier the materialization.

In conclusion, you should tell nobody what the words on the cards mean or give anyone any suggestion as to what you are trying to accomplish. Just keep it to yourself. Any outside ridicule or criticism can be detrimental to your success with these methods.

How to Use Telepathy to Meet Men

Telepathy is the sending and receiving of thought messages without words being spoken. Thoughts pass from your mind to anothers mind through a sea of electrons which surround us. Thought is a real thing just like any visible object. Thought sends out vibrations just as light and heat do, but much more intense.

To employ this method, you will simply be looking in the direction of a man and you will be sending forth positive thought images, conveying a message such as, "I would like to meet you." While sending the message you will be looking at him with a steady gaze.

The eye is an important factor in influencing people. It has the power of impressing your will upon another. In using this method, you will need to develop a magnetic gaze. To develop the magnetic gaze, practice the following exercise:

Stand in front of a large mirror with your face about 15 inches from it. You can also use a small mirror placed on a table. Using ink, make a small dot at the base of your nose, squarely between your eyes. Focus your eyes upon the dot, while staring in the mirror, and gaze at it firmly without winking. If you get the urge to wink, just raise your eyelids a little and this should prevent you from winking. Keep practicing this until you can gaze at the mirror without winking for about fifteen

How to Meet Men Using the Powers of the Mind

seconds.

While using this magnetic gaze, a man will either react positively or he will break the gaze coming from you. If he won't look at you, you'll have to assume perhaps that he might not be interested in you. However, you may want to just try harder. If he responds to your gaze and your silent message, you will soon see the results.

Now, I will describe how to use these telepathic powers.

First of all, don't let your mind wander while you are trying to make contact with a man. Concentrate all your thoughts on the task at hand.

Pick out a man and give him your magnetic gaze. While looking at him send out a thought such as, "That man over there wants to talk to me" or "That man over there is dying to meet me." You can make your own messages to send, these are just examples. Just repeat your message over and over in your mind in a relaxed manner and make your message short and to the point.

Don't tell others you are using mental telepathy to influence others. Their skepticism or ridicule may weaken your faith.

Also, you must not use this power to bring harm to others or to send unkind thoughts.

That's all there is to it. Using this method, you can make contact with a man without uttering a single word. With practice, men will receive your thoughts and act upon them. Just imagine how much fun it will be, controlling the thoughts of men and being able to influence a man with your mind. After you have learned how to use mental telepathy, you will be able to actually will a man to get up and come over and talk to you.

In conclusion, try this method and you will find yourself meeting more men.

CHAPTER FIFTEEN

10 Cities With the Most Available Single Men

As stated by a Princeton University survey, here are the top 10 cities in the United States with the most eligible bachelors.

* **LOS ANGELES** - This town attracts many aspiring models and actresses. These women come from all over the United States in hopes of breaking into the movies, show business, or becoming a top model. To make a long story short, this town is loaded with beautiful and talented women. Then on top of it you have your local beautiful California girls.

All these lovelies attract single men to come to live in Los Angeles. Thus, there is quite an abundance of nice, attractive men here.

* **HOUSTON** - Being that I live in Houston, I'm quite an authority on the large number of men here.

This is the oil capital and petro-chemical center of the United States, not to mention the Johnson Space Center which is loaded with engineers and professional men.

There's a lot of wealth here and real good-paying jobs. So

10 Cities With the Most Available Single Men

the men are well-to-do and believe me, there's plenty of them.

Also, back in the 70's when the rest of country was in a recession and Houston was not because of the "oil boom", this attracted a lot of men here from the rest of the U.S. seeking employment and wealth. If you're ever in Houston hit some of the nightclubs in the Clear Lake area. The odds run anywhere from three to ten men per women.

* **WASHINGTON, D.C.** - The key to the large number of men here is the military. You have the Pentagon and military bases which have a lot of men at the professional level.

Of course, you have a lot of men, too, in government positions. Some of which are high-paying positions.

* **SAN FRANCISCO** - I know what you're thinking. Aren't most of the men in San Francisco gay? Studies have shown that 40% of the single male population is gay.

Don't let this mislead you though. There's the other 60% who aren't gay. Still there's an overwhelming amount of men that come to live in the Bay Area because this area is literally a "paradise." The beauty of the mountains, ocean, and lifestyle are very attractive to these men. So they come here in large numbers.

* **SAN JOSE** - Men come here in droves because of the employment opportunities in this California city. There's a lot of high-tech positions here.

* **SEATTLE** - Because of the natural beauty surrounding Seattle, a lot of outdoor type of men are attracted to this city. Also, this is a very cultural oriented city and very modern.

There's an enormous amount of bars and a good nightlife. Also, plenty of good restaurants.

Finally, it's a very sports oriented city with the Seahawks and the Washington Huskies.

* **SAN DIEGO** - Do you like servicemen? This town is literally overrun by the military. You have 25% of the entire U.S. Navy here. Also, throw in 20% of the entire Marine Corp too. So you're looking at around 115,000+ military personnel.

These guys are super lonely and a lot of them are away from home. Females are very much in demand here and you will be very popular.

* **NEW ORLEANS** - This city came in fourth in the Princeton study. There are three eligible men for every four women. Talk about the odds being in your favor!

* **FT. LAUDERDALE** - Well you've heard the song, "Where the Boys Are" by Connie Francis. This song is really about Ft. Lauderdale. This town is inhabited by thousands of college men at Spring Break (especially Spring Break).

I highly recommend to make it a point to take a vacation annually here at Spring Break. Once you see thousands of handsome hunks, you'll swear that you're in heaven. And you probably are. One think is for sure. You will have the time of your life. Guaranteed!

* **DENVER** - There are much, much more men here than women. The reason being because of the skiing recreation industry. The slopes are packed with lots of single men.

Skiing really attracts the men to Denver area. Also, the ski lodges and pubs are full of men.

So, why don't you plan a ski trip to this area at least once a year. You will have a great time on the slopes, not to mention all the men that you will meet.

"100 WAYS TO MEET AND ATTRACT MEN"

1. MOST OF YOU CHIEFLY NEED ENCOURAGEMENT TO TRY. Go out and try to meet and interest men at all of the varied places where men and women come together. Most women who are unsuccessful in love and romance chiefly need ego-bolstering and suggestions of places to look.
2. INDIVIDUAL DIFFERENCES - EVERY WOMAN IS ATTRACTIVE TO SOME MEN. Both men and women who might be considered unattractive to the average person succeed in attracting and winning highly desirable mates every day, everywhere. Your own experience will suggest many such cases. Taste and preference in love is infinite. Here is an important fact for you. Believe it and act on it! There is no woman who would not be attractive and desirable to at least some men, including some gorgeous men who would knock your eyes out, and who you ordinarily, though quite foolishly, wouldn't dare to approach.
3. FIND OUT WHAT IMPRESSION YOU MAKE ON MEN. Get an honest and accurate viewpoint from your friends on how you act around men. You just may be coming across as stuck up, sarcastic, domineering, mean, angry, pessimistic, or dull, but once you get a clear picture of how men are seeing you, you can make the appropriate changes.
4. THOUSANDS OF NICE MEN ARE READY TO GIVE THEMSELVES TO THE FIRST WOMAN WHO IS SENSITIVE, SYMPATHETIC, AND UNDERSTANDING. Loneliness, feelings of inner emptiness, a yearning for a sense of personal importance are so universal that millions of nice men, single and married, are psychologically ready to throw themselves, passionately and completely, at the first woman who shows them tenderness, affection, devotion...at the first woman who makes them feel wanted, loved, important, and lovable!
5. ANY SPECIAL ASSET OR TALENT gives you higher percentage, but you can succeed in love without any of them, if necessary, provided you have confidence in yourself.
6. MOST WOMEN ARE DEFEATED BY EGO-DEFEATING IMAGINATIONS BEFORE THEY HAVE EVEN BEGUN. The fear that you will not be liked, that you haven't got a chance, that it's no use even trying because "he" could never possibly go for

FINDING MR. RIGHT

you are your chief, self-imposed obstacles. You use your imagination to erect barriers and obstacles rather than help your cause!

7. A MAGIC FORMULA IF YOU BELIEVE AND PRACTICE IT: A famous, amazingly successful New York psychologist once said during an interview: "I tell all my shy inhibited, introverted patients: Never be afraid to *ask,* You will be surprised and delighted to find out how often you receive a Yes! It is the expectation of receiving a "No" which defeats most women "on the make" before they have half-started."

8. DON'T BE AFRAID TO ASK HIM!

9. A GUARANTEED TECHNIQUE FOR MEETING ATTRACTIVE MEN EVERY DAY EVERYWHERE. Try this: Make it your business, a self-imposed compulsion and obligation, to talk to at least three attractive, single, men every day wherever you happen to see them, whenever the fancy strikes you. If you want amazing results, don't limit yourself to three. Force yourself to start a conversation, to try and meet a dozen or more men every day, wherever and however you happen to come in contact with them.

10. YOU CAN NOT LEARN MERELY BY READING, YOU MUST GO OUT AND PRACTICE THIS: If you see a man on the street, looking in the window of a store, waiting for a bus, sitting on a train, in the next aisle of a movie, shopping in a department store, and for any reason this man appeals to you, strike up a conversation, start talking to him about anything that comes to mind.

11. HOW DO YOU START A CONVERSATION WITH A STRANGER? If your manner and speech expresses friendliness, openness, lack of ulterior motives, almost any opening or overture on your part will frequently meet with an appreciative response. By the law of averages, you are certain to come across many men so eager for companionship that they will be happy to respond to you.

12. STARTING WITH WHAT IS "APPROPRIATE" AND "NATURAL": For example, if you are in a movie, what can be more natural than to ask a question about a picture, or make a

100 Ways to Meet and Attract Men

comment on your reaction to it, or ask the man beside you how he feels about it. If you are on the street, you can always make a comment on something both of you happen to be looking at, or ask for the time, a match, for information on the nearest movie, restaurant, or subway. Then depending upon his reaction, you can always *invite him to join you!*

13. EVEN THE WORLD'S OLDEST PICK-UP LINE OFTEN WORKS. When by chance you approach the right man, almost anything you say will work. Even the oldest, crazy opening line, "Haven't we met some place before?" is used successfully every hour of the day in developing exciting romantic relationships.

14. DO NOT OVERLOOK ANY CHANNEL FOR MEETING MEN. Until you find what you want and are satisfied, you must use every possible and conceivable channel for meeting men. A list of places are suggested in this book.

15. EVERY DATE - EVERY MAN - CAN HELP YOU DEVELOP MORE SKILL AND POLISH. Every man you meet and go out with can richly add to your experience and self-development if you look upon it in this way. Don't bury yourself in a movie on the first date. Talk to him about himself, draw out all his interests, desires, crucial life experiences. Share your own experiences with him. From each man you can learn to speak more fluently, with greater ease; you can learn more about the psychology of man; you can develop increasing skill in making him like you and in enjoying your company.

16. MAKE YOURSELF SENSITIVE TO HIS NEEDS. Try to feel and understand just what makes him "tick." Try, occasionally, to put yourself in his shoes mentally and *empathize* with his attitudes and view of life. As you sense unfulfilled needs on his part, really try to satisfy them. Does he want tenderness? Companionship? Boldness? does he urgently want to get married and will an early subtle indication of serious intentions create the best impression?

17. GIVE FLATTERING ATTENTION PRECISELY WHERE HE MOST CRAVES IT. Does he know he is handsome? Then perhaps he would most appreciate subtle compliments on his intelligence and charm. Is he plain, or suffering from an un-

deserved sense of inferiority? Then he may most appreciate any compliments which are deft enough to be believable, on the attractiveness of his hair, eyes, physique, or posture.

Explore him and feel him out conversationally, then give flattering attention and appreciation not to his strong points (where he usually does not need it) but on his weak points.

18. LOOK FOR HIS SORE SPOT, HIS UNFULFILLED NEEDS, HIS AREAS OF INFERIORITY OR INADEQUACY, AND STRIVE TO MAKE HIM FEEL GOOD THERE!

19. WHAT IT MEANS TO BE A GOOD LISTENER: A good listener is not really passive. You have to give your fullest, most intense attention to him: physically, mentally, emotionally; by your facial expressions, posture, your voice and comments. You have to like him and be genuinely interested. Be sensitive enough to discover that every human being has beautiful, lovable inner qualities if you seek for them. Encourage and stimulate the continued flow of his conversation by asking questions, making comments, expressing interest and appreciation for what he is saying. Be ready, too, to contribute your own feelings, experiences, knowledge as it bears upon what he is expressing.

20. IT'S EASY TO BE A GOOD LISTENER IF HE'S VOLUBLE, BUT WHAT IF HE FINDS IT HARD TO CONVERSE EASILY? If he's shy, inhibited, reticent, draw him out. Make him feel important, comfortable, relaxed and appreciated. Your own spontaneity, informality and complete interest in him will bring him out of it.

21. IF YOU NEED TO DEVELOP YOUR OWN SPONTANEITY AND EMOTIONAL FREEDOM, STUDY REFLEX THERAPY BY ANDREW SALTER: Creative Press, NY.

22. THREE BASIC ATTITUDES WHICH FORM A GOLDEN KEY IN ALL HUMAN RELATIONSHIPS IF PRACTICED AND LIVED: Every man wants, unconsciously yearns for, three basic attitudes from the woman he will love. But for that matter, every human being needs and deserves and will grow in power when he receives these feelings from another person. The formula is: Give a man you desire, *faith, acceptance,* and *respect.* Believe in him, trust him, find the good, beautiful and

uniquely admirable within him. Search for it. It is always there! It really makes me sad to think of all the men that are ignored or even dumped prematurely because a woman just did not take the time to get to know him on the inside.

Accept him as he is. This does not mean accepting his pretensions, false fronts or unrealistic goals and dreams. But accept him as he is deep down in his own best and most natural self. Respect him completely in your motives, manners, speech, actions, and plans. If you can truly develop and cultivate these attitudes in yourself, the most desirable men in the world will be eagerly available to you!

23. THE POWER OF "RESPECTFUL AGGRESSIVENESS" IN LOVE-MAKING: "She who hesitates is lost!" is often too sadly true of the would-be-lover. Aggressiveness, assertiveness, courage, and persistence are often essential in meeting the man you want and in developing a satisfying love affair. This is not to say that *brutal* aggressiveness or boorish assertiveness are recommended. But you must be aggressive enough to start the action and pursue it, even if given little encouragement initially, unless you are definitely and decisively refused. But that is rare. Don't look for rejection. Don't expect failure! You have to exercise enough assertiveness to keep moving forward, from asking a man for a date, or beginning a conversation with a stranger, through all the successive stages.

24. WHY SOME WOMEN NEVER GET PAST FIRST BASE: Many women with every advantage in looks, personality, and genuine affection of the men they court, never get very far in developing a love affair simply because they do not keep trying, do not keep moving forward. Ignore mild rebuffs, even repeated refusals, unless you are quite certain that the man *really* wants you to stop! Even then, unless he indicates plainly otherwise, you can always try again next time! Remember that most of the time he is only waiting for the opportunity to join you in love and sex if, in the process, you can make him feel secure and appreciated.

25. GOOD ADVICE IS PLENTIFUL - BUT HOW DO YOU TAKE ADVANTAGE OF IT? The advice and ideas contained in this book may be uniquely invaluable to you, but only if you

can apply it. There are plenty of other good books and articles which people read, enjoy and ignore! How can you make this advice to change into a more dynamic, effective person with the opposite sex?

26. DON'T JUST READ IT ONCE. No truly worthwhile nonfiction book can be read quickly only once to maximum advantage. You should read, re-read, study, meditate upon, and practice daily, every idea and suggestion in this book which appeals to you.

27. ALL LEARNING IS SELF-DISCOVERY. The human race learned a great deal about the philosophy of effective living thousands of years ago, but each individual must re-discover these truths for herself, make them her own self-discoveries, or they mean nothing to her.

I urge you to re-read and study intensively every word in this book and systematically, persistently, patiently practice it in life, daily, at every possible opportunity. Furthermore, every time you try to meet a man, start a conversation with a stranger, develop a close, affectionate relationship, *think about* what happened afterwards as this book bears upon what occurred. Analyze for yourself what went wrong, what went right, and try to analyze *why*. Only in this way will you use this book for continuous self-improvement and more effective personal development in finding, attracting, and winning men.

28. OTHER BOOKS CAN HELP IF YOU STUDY AND MASTER THEM. In addition to this book, there are many other books which can be tremendously helpful to you, which can help you more fully understand and appreciate some of the ideas in this book if their fullest significance has escaped you, but you must use them the way we recommend: Study, re-read, master, think seriously about, and practice their advice in life, daily, and persistently.

A Small Sampling of Some of These Helpful Books Follows:

29. HOW TO WIN FRIENDS AND INFLUENCE PEOPLE by Dale Carnegie. This old classic on how to be popular and get

along with people is still available in pocket book form in any book store and is a fantastic handbook if you *believe* it and *live* it!

30. FLYING SOLO by Kenneth Wydro. Being single is often a time for self-doubt; but it can and should be a time to grow, to expand, to soar. Flying Solo proves that the choice is within you to make, and it shows you how it's done: from the bar scene to the job, from your spiritual self to your financial self, from breaking up with style to finding a lifetime mate.

31. CONTACT, THE FIRST FOUR MINUTES by Leonard Zunin, M.D. with Natalie Zunin. This book was written to help you dissolve the distance between yourself and others. One of its main goals is to inspire you to new awareness of who you are and how you present yourself. Through techniques for sensing more about yourself and others you can develop more control over the first four minutes of any contact situation. Your relationships can be warmer, closer, and more significant, if you wish.

32. SHYNESS by Dr. Phillip Zimbardo. Dr. Phillip Zimbardo brings together the results of five years of extensive study, the experiences of more than 5000 people and the startlingly successful techniques of his revolutionary Shyness Clinic to help you face and conquer this life-limiting problem.

33. HOW TO BE SINGLE CREATIVELY by Charles Fracchia. Serves as a guide and a catalyst for the creative experience of living a single life in the fullest possible sense.

34. READ THE BASIC WRITINGS OF SIGMUND FREUD and any other modern psychology books which will help you better understand the dynamics and motivations of human beings, help you understand more sensitively and fully what makes a man tick, and how to sense and gratify his special needs.

35. A PRIMARY PRINCIPLE OF EMOTIONAL HEALTH AND MATURITY. In addition, you should read as many modern books on sex technique as you can get your hands on. You will find at least some helpful things in all of them. But, keep this in mind: if you ever find anything in these books on sex, love, marriage, etc. which makes you feel guilty, ashamed, inadequate or worried about your "normality", either you have grossly

misinterpreted the book or the book contains some real sheer nonsense which you had best disregard!

IF you read the enlightened modern books on sex and psychology, you will learn that acceptance of your body and all its functions, and ability to respect, accept and enjoy many avenues of sexual gratification are a primary principle of mental and emotional health and maturity.

36. IF YOU USE THE LAW OF PROBABILITIES, YOU DON'T HAVE TO CHANGE ONE IOTA! If you make it your business to constantly go where and be where many men congregate, and if you put all your efforts into trying to meet and go out with as many men as possible, you will sooner or later meet a man who will fulfill all your dreams and will fall in love with you exactly as you are no matter what handicaps you may think you possess. Individual differences and variations in taste are so great that there are men who are attracted to ugly women, crippled women, fat women, women with eccentricities and peculiarities. If you utilize the law of probabilities of chance and make it your urgent task to meet and go out with one hundred men, for example, long before you have met your one hundredth man, in most cases, you will have found at least one, but more probably, *many* men who will be strongly attracted to you and who will find you irresistible, no matter who you are, no matter what you are like.

37. A FEW TIPS ON SEX APPEAL AND ATTRACTIVENESS FOR WINNING THE CONVENTIONAL MAN. Most ordinary, healthy men are fairly predictable on the constituents of initial sex appeal. These hints are aimed at increasing your percentage with the average man.

Unless you're decidedly pretty and well-built, you will make a more attractive impression, enhance your sex appeal, if you rely on extreme neatness, cleanliness, and good dress. Even a homely woman with a flabby physique can look proud, popular and attractive if she gives meticulous, and expensive attention to being well clothed. Buy the most expensive dresses, outfits, pants, blouses, etc. that you can afford. The cheap ones may fill up your wardrobe but never give you the best break in attractiveness.

You don't have to know anything about clothes really. Go to a clothing store with an excellent reputation and place yourself in the hands of the saleswoman. They have enough experience and practice to pick out the kinds of clothes which will make the most flattering combinations for you. Almost every book on salesmanship goes into detail on this facet. You are interested in selling yourself - selling your personality, attractiveness and desirability to men. Take the same advice!

Read Vogue magazine, Harper's Bazaar, and other women's magazines which devote much of their space to discussion and display of smart current fashions for women.

If, however, you are willing to play for the Law of Probabilities, this advice is less important. If you have outstanding physical and personality assets, it is also far less important.

38. POSTURE AND SEX APPEAL. Posture and manner can contribute greatly to sex appeal, or conversely, diminish it. You may have noticed that some men can appear much more attractive and sexually desirable than their looks alone would warrant because of the sex appeal they convey thru posture, voice, smile, vigor of personality. The same is equally true of women.

39. THE WEST POINT MODEL. If you have a sloppy posture, an awkward walk, a slumped, flabby way of carrying yourself, attention to more erect, vigorous, confident, assertive posture can make you many times more attractive and persuasive to the opposite sex. Don't be afraid to practice in front of a mirror. Practice walking with your head up, your chin in, your back erect, your chest as far out as you can push it, and your belly sucked in tight!

Merely standing and walking in this way is terrifically beneficial exercise. But, it is also ever effective in magnifying your sex appeal. Think of the West Point posture as a general pattern model and then develop a posture pattern of your own which is more natural for you, but further in the West Point posture direction than what you possess now.

40. THE POWER OF SETTING GOALS. Every time you give yourself a modest, attainable goal, but one which does require

some *effort* and some *courage*, and you accomplish it, you build another pound of confidence into your bones, flesh and fiber and nervous system - where it must grow and develop if it is to be genuine and durable.

How do you start? Give yourself a small immediate goal and carry it out. Then go on to bigger and better things. If you are afraid of men, go out with any man, and every man, as often as you can. Each time, pat yourself on the back mentally and feel yourself grow more relaxed and secure in the company of men. Set a goal of getting a date with the single man in your place of employment and ask him! Whether he accepts or turns you down, at least be gratified that you were able to carry through, the action of asking him to go out and trying to get a date for yourself on your own.

If you have a phone number in your address book of a single eligible man, call him up and talk to him, ask him for a date. Even if you have never seen him, even if you saw him a long time ago and didn't hit it off, even if he has already refused you, make yourself call him up and try again.

Set yourself a goal of talking to a strange man on the subway, bus, elevator, or street, today! Even if it never gets further than a few casual comments exchanged between you, it will build your confidence and skill and prepare you for more ambitious goals next time. You build confidence by doing in small ways and forcing yourself forward to gradually bigger and bigger goals.

41. IF EMOTIONAL BLOCKS TO MEETING MEN ARE TOO STRONG FOR SELF-HELP, DON'T BE AFRAID TO TRY PSYCHOTHERAPY OR TRANQUILIZERS. Some of you women who read this may be so shy, inhibited, and psychologically blocked that you will be unable to truly profit from the advice contained in this book. I beseech you not to come to any such conclusion until you have first made a strong, persistent effort to practice these ideas. Remember that the overwhelming majority of people who read this will be able to use this advice effectively without outside profession help.

But if you have powerful blocks, can not bear to start a conversation with a man, or even face the company of a date, no matter how hard you try, then you probably need psychotherapeutic help.

Get in touch with the nearest mental hygiene clinic, or ask your family physician to recommend a good psychiatrist or psychologist. Your physician may also prescribe one of the many, very effective tranquilizers, not as a cure-all, but to help reduce your anxiety, embarrassment and fear sufficiently for you to begin going out, meeting people, talking to them, and developing promising relationships.

42. YOUR DAILY NEWSPAPER AND BEING AN INTERESTING CONVERSATIONALIST. In addition to being a good listener, a wide-range of interesting topics, comments and humor are helpful in making yourself an attractive, fluent conversationalist with men.

Your daily newspaper can help in this task. Instead of just browsing through it in ten or fifteen minutes each day, read your favorite newspaper from page to page, thoroughly. Read, think about what you are reading, and remember everything of interest and personal importance as you go through each section of the paper. As you read, rehearse in your own mind which items will make an interesting story, an amusing anecdote, a situation which relates to your own and his previous experiences, an item you can modify and include in your repertoire of jokes, witticisms, wisecracks, etc. The human interest stories, even the gossip columns, can often be fruitful sources for vivid, amusing conversation with the appropriate man.

43. LIFE IS FOR NOW! Regardless of the frustrations, failures and grief you may have experienced in the past, there is no reason to permit yourself to be chained to the past, or for that matter, to be so concerned with dreams about the future that the present passes you by.

Life is here, now, this moment...to *live*, to see and feel intensely, to enjoy, to make new starts, new beginnings, build a new life. You can begin actions this very moment which will begin to change you for the better, make you more attractive to, and successful with, the opposite sex. Act, within and without, with friendliness, confidence, and intense interest in others.

Like people, even while remaining very open-eyed about their failings and shortcomings. Feel this affection for people inside you and act upon it and you will begin to change internally and externally in a direction which is infinitely more attractive and charming to men.

44. USE IMAGINATION, CREATIVITY AND EMOTIONAL DRIVE IN MEETING AND "MAKING" HANDSOME MEN. Don't rely upon the most convenient, ready at hand methods, sources and techniques. Put some energy, imagination and hard work into the task. Some of the techniques which follow and some of the suggested sources may seem obvious and prosaic when stated in simple, brief form. But it is up to you to go beyond the ordinary, usual approach to these sources for meeting men.

For example, you can go to a dance almost every day and *never dance*, yet still meet dozens of attractive men! Try this: Go up to any man at the dance or nightclub, who is alone and available, as if you were going to ask him for a dance, but instead, in your own words, sincerely, say something like this: "I would love to ask you to dance with me, but I'm not going to because I can't dance! I just had to meet you. Would you mind sitting this one out and just talk and get acquainted?" You will be amazed at how often this works with the most desirable men.

Here Are a Few Examples of How Imagination and Courage Can be Applied

45. MEET NEW MEN IN YOUR LOCAL NEWSPAPERS. If you see a picture and a local news item about a man who appeals to you while perusing your newspaper, cut out his picture and the item. In the newspapers of small communities these items can contain the addresses and pictures of handsome, eligible men in connection with every conceivable kind of event. Get the address right out of the paper and send him a letter introducing yourself and ask if you could get together for lunch or meet for a drink.

If you have some strong obvious ties in common, mention it in your letter, or better yet, just call him up on the phone. For example, if your families know each other, if by chance you went to the same school, if you happen to belong to the same church or organizations, have the same hobbies and interests, use these as stepping stones, as channels to an introduction!

46. GET YOUR CIRCLE OF FRIENDS AND ACQUAINTANCES TO HELP. This, too, often takes some nerve, though less of it than for the above technique but is also very effective. Ask all your friends, acquaintances, associates, relatives, and neighbors, to give you the names, addresses and phone numbers, if not direct introductions, to any and every single, young man they know. Then call them up or write them, introduce yourself, start a conversation and ask for a date. Be as friendly, warm and informal as you can manage. Try it with persistence. Don't get discouraged five dozen times. By the time you are starting on your sixty-first, you will get marvelous results!

47. GET A PART-TIME JOB WHERE YOU ARE BOUND TO MEET A LOT OF MEN. Even if you now have a very good job, consider trying this: Get yourself a temporary part-time job, evenings, weekends, or whenever you have spare time, regardless of salary or previous background, where you will come into constant contact with men. Department store sales jobs are ideal for this purpose, but almost any selling job, even canvassing can be helpful both in building your confidence in meeting and dealing with people, and in actually giving you more opportunity to meet attractive men from much wider horizons than your own neighborhood or job might provide.

When you get this part-time job, strike up conversations with every single man you meet who interests you. Don't worry about your job or your earnings. You aren't doing the work for a living or a future career anyway. Use the job in a way which will help you develop constant new sources of male contacts.

Here Are 29 Additional Ways of Meeting Men

48. TAKE ADVANTAGE OF DANCES IN YOUR COMMUNITY. Square dances are particularly useful because everyone seems to be a little bit more relaxed, comfortable, and in small country towns everybody knows everyone, and so this is

not like the big city nightclubs where people are uptight, so the greater informality makes it easier for you to meet someone. But, don't forget that most men come to dances to meet women and not necessarily to dance. You really do not need to know how to dance to meet many handsome, available men at dances.

49. PARTICIPATE IN COMMUNITY CHEST DRIVES AND COMMUNITY ACTIVITIES OF ALL KINDS. Offer your services. You will meet fellow solicitors; you will meet people on your calls.

50. ATTEND ADULT EDUCATION CLASSES. Some lonely, bored, frustrated men go there to meet women or to escape from their daily routine, than go there to learn.

51. JOIN A POLITICAL CLUB in your community. Have you seen all those available men at campaign rallies and political conventions? Become active politically, on the local level, and you can meet desirable men.

52. MEET NEW FRIENDS THROUGH CORRESPONDENCE. Pen pals and correspondence clubs are pleasant ways to meet men from an almost unlimited source. You can practically have your pick of any part of the country and any "ideal type" you have in mind. You can answer ads or place your own in magazines and tabloids.

53. If you live in a rural area, participate in GRANGE MEETINGS to develop friendships.

54. If you play GOLF or you are willing to learn how, you can go to public links where you can be matched in foursomes of both sexes. Combine health, fun and man-chasing!

55. Most people meet and marry others who have a great deal in common. You can seek out a NATIONALITY ORGANIZATION in your area. Are you of Irish, Greek, or Italian descent? You will be welcomed in a Nationality Club of your choice.

56. BOWLING has become an effective an universal means for men and women to meet. Look into joining a bowling league where the teams are made up of both males and females.

57. GET IN THE SWIM. Be sure, whatever you do, to visit the indoor pools in the winter and even more important, visit the

outdoor pools in the summer. If you're good, there's always an attractive man who wants to improve his stroke. In the water, formality is dropped. It's easy to get acquainted. Take my word for it, people tend to be more friendly in the water. So, take advantage of this fact and approach men.

58. BECOME A RED CROSS VOLUNTEER. Help during drives, serve in hospitals, teach first-aid courses to others. Widen your circle of friends.

59. JOIN A LOCAL AMATEUR BAND OR ORCHESTRA if you play an instrument. People who work together or play together become good friends.

60. Join in good times with your fellow sports enthusiasts by greater participation in ROLLER SKATING and ICE SKATING.

61. There are opportunities for social as well as spiritual betterment at church-sponsored socials, fund drives, the choir, etc.

62. MUSIC LOVER? Attend free municipal concerts. Also get tickets to any private concerts in your area. During intermission you can discuss the program with attractive men who share your interest. You can try to sit beside unescorted men who will happily exchange comments - which may lead to phone numbers and dates.

63. There is something about travel away from home which makes both sexes friendlier, less inhibited, more aggressive in going after anyone who attracts them. If you can arrange it, take trips by plane, ship, bus...leave your car at home!

64. INTERESTED IN THEATRE? Amateur theatrical groups are usually easy to join if you can act, build sets, sell tickets, write scripts, operate lights, etc.

65. In most large cities, your newspapers or yellow pages lists MARRIAGE BROKERS who introduce romance-seekers for a fee.

66. JOIN A HOBBY CLUB. If you play cards, chess, checkers, you will find public and private clubs where you can spend enjoyable evenings and meet pleasant partners of both sexes.

67. If this activity appeals to you, join a HIKING, BICYCLING,

FINDING MR. RIGHT

OR HOSTEL CLUB in your area. Overnight trips, robust fun, informal social fun! You really get to know each other by sharing an activity and romances can be formed.

68. HOW ABOUT A VACATION RESORT? There are combinations to fit any pocketbook. Many single men and women go to resort hotels in their states only for the weekends. You can go to Florida and the Catskills; to Las Vegas or New England, etc. Frequent weekends at the same hotel will make you feel at home with a large crowd of new friends.

69. Make friends on the trail through HORSEBACK RIDING. If you don't know how, consider taking lessons.

70. How long has it been since you had a large FAMILY REUNION? You can meet new distant relatives or induce relatives to introduce you to attractive single eligible men they know.

71. VOLUNTEER your services to CIVIL DEFENSE ORGANIZATIONS which have become increasingly more active and urgently need help.

72. Check your newspapers and phone books for PROFESSIONAL SOCIAL CLUBS which introduce people and arrange get-acquainted parties as a business.

73. Get yourself a racquet and meet friends on the TENNIS COURTS!

74. If you like to paint, or have always wanted to learn, join a PAINTING GROUP or club...You'll find both sexes, all ages, and all types of wielding brushes.

75. LOOK INTO OTHER HOBBIES. Look into your own interests. Read hobby magazines. Find a hobby group in which you can cultivate a new or old interest and meet many men and women interested in similar pursuits.

76. LOOK INTO OTHER SPORTS. For example, archery, gymnastics, volley ball, competitive diving, ping pong, boating, etc. If you are good at one, you will be attractive to other participants of the opposite sex. You will have a natural common interest on the basis on which friendships, even lifetime matings, may develop.

Here Are Some Suggestions on Technique, Personality, and Miscellaneous Hints:

77. HOW TO CHARM ANY MAN INTO FALLING IN LOVE: There are women who have such winning personalities, such conquering charm, that they can practically seduce a "blind date" over the phone. By analyzing both women who most, and women who least, possess the vital ingredient of "sex appeal" charm, we can present a few of the principles by which it is done. However, this doesn't mean you can equal their charm overnight merely by reading about it. You will have to find your own ways, develop your own brand of charm, and utilizing these principles in a manner which is both polished, and convincing for you.
78. Make the man feel that he's the most important person in the world.
79. Make him feel like he's worth a million dollars.
80. Make him feel attractive, gorgeous, wanted, and sexy.
81. Shower him with attention.
82. Keep talking to him about himself. Forget about yourself.
83. DON'T EVER LEAVE HIM ALONE! Send him cards, flowers, candy, telegrams, gifts, phone him constantly, see him as often as possible until you achieve your objectives.
84. SHOW HIM THAT YOU CARE, DEEPLY, INTENSELY, FOR ALWAYS by the way you look at him, talk to him, pursue him, and listen to him.
85. STRIVE TO MAKE HIM FEEL GOOD whenever he is in your presence, when talking with you, and when out on a date. This means showing him a good time, telling him jokes and interesting anecdotes, expressing appreciation of his sense of humor, behaving as if everything he utters is a bright gem.
86. MAKE HIM DEPENDENT UPON YOU. Make him miss you when you are not around. Teach him to find you more and more essential by being a real friend, an interesting and dependable companion, a reliable antidote to loneliness, a continuous part of his life and thought.
87. MEET HIS FAMILY as soon as possible and treat them as if they were royalty. Get his family on your side in persuading him

of your charm and desirability.

88. OCCASIONALLY BE UNPREDICTABLE! Many men, however much they value reliability and security in their woman, also tend to take for granted, and to undervalue a woman who is too ordinary, too conformist, too dependably predictable. Don't do it too often, and don't hurt him needlessly, but occasionally demonstrate unpredictable and unexpected qualities.

Leave at least a slight touch of mystery and romantic secrecy about your innermost self. For example, suddenly take a trip without advance warning and write to him from your temporary distant stopping point. Take him on a date to some place he has never been before and which he could not have expected from your previous behavior. Use your imagination to display other romantic touches of mystery and unpredictability. For another example, you may suddenly send him a present which opens up a completely unsuspected but attractive facet of yourself to his admiring contemplation.

89. LOFTY, DRIVING AMBITION IS ATTRACTIVE TO SOME MEN. Spin beautiful dreams of the future for him, and weave him into them! Express your highest, most dramatic ambitions and goals to him, Express them vividly, as concretely and confidently as possible. Give him the feeling that he will go along with you and share the heights, the glory, the success, and your mutual happiness.

90. WHAT TO TELL HIM ONCE YOU HAVE GAINED HIS RESPECT AND HAVE BEGUN TO MEAN SOMETHING TO HIM. Once a man begins to like you, he usually wants to be told certain things over and over about himself. Sad to say, many frustrated husbands, as well as single men, yearn to hear this from their wives but never do. Even where they are *really* loved they are often grossly insulted by being taken for granted.

Tell him over and over again, as sincerely as you can, in as many different ways as you can phrase it that: "He's wonderful. He's the most important person in the world to you. You love him. You want him." Once a man *really likes you*, he never, never tires of hearing these things eternally.

91. HOW TO LEARN "SEX CHARM TECHNIQUE" FROM A

100 Ways to Meet and Attract Men

MOVIE! Most psychologists would agree that it is far better to *be yourself*; to put your effort into self-improvement and self-development. But if you are too fearful and depressed by a sense of failure and inadequacy to trust to the cultivation of your own most effective self, you may prefer this idea. It's yours to use or omit as you wish. Many single women have found it extremely effective:

Pick out a movie star (or character in literature) whom you admire and with whom you can identify. Go to all of her pictures (or read and re-read every book about her). When you find this movie idol in a love story where she plays the romantic lead and displays her man-swooning charm to greatest advantage, see that picture over and over again until you have learned and mastered every nuance of her voice, speech, manner, humor, posture, all the elements in her screen personality which contribute to her man-conquering style...and pattern yourself accordingly.

92. PICK OUT A SUCCESSFUL MAN-KILLER IN YOUR CROWD AND STUDY HER STYLE. Don't ask her questions. She probably doesn't know herself how she does it. But try to go on "man-hunting expeditions" with her. Go to dances, nightclubs, parties, the beach, with her. Try to arrange some double dates together. Take advantage of every opportunity to watch her in action and study intensively. Remember to rehearse in your own mind, every line and gesture.

93. KEEP A DAILY JOURNAL FOR NEW IDEAS IN IMPROVING YOUR OWN TECHNIQUE. If you keep your eyes and ears open, you will see women pick meet men and interest them, you will read items about how romances and love affairs were started and developed in the daily newspapers, movie magazines, novels, and general magazines.

94. WORK OUT A PERSONAL "LINE" AND TRY IT WITH ENDLESS VARIATIONS. Some women need the support, the crutch, of a definite "line" in approaching and winning a man. If you do, give a good deal of thought to this while you're working, reading, traveling. Formulate a number of possibly effective lines in your mind and then sit down with a pencil and paper and write them down. Practice them out loud in front of a mirror until you

get just the phraseology which sounds most natural, smooth, spontaneous and attractive. Practice delivering it in private aloud until you can use it as if it has just occurred to you in response to this particular man. Go out and practice it, but with the freedom and confidence to vary it imaginatively to fit every new situation and man.

95. WHY SOME OF THE SUGGESTIONS ARE CONTRADICTORY. You can't be spontaneous and natural, cultivate your own deeper self and also imitate the style of sexy starlets. Some of the advice on these pages is, of necessity, inconsistent and contradictory. The reason is: You are a unique individual. You have been supplied with a tremendous range of suggestions and ideas. Many will not appeal to you or seem appropriate. Some will seem to be the answer to your prayers. You must feel free to choose any and all which you "feel" can be most valuable, and feel equally free to discard and ignore any and all others which do not seem right for you personally.

96. SOME MEN CRAVE A WOMAN WHO IS DOMINATING AND EVEN A LITTLE BIT CRUEL! We mentioned before the importance of sensitively exploring the unfulfilled needs of the man you have met. At times, in the nature of being just a wee bit unpredictable and complex, you may act dominating, bossy, even slightly sadistic. Watch his reactions closely when you do! If you see a glint in his eyes, a pleasurable submissiveness, as suddenly more positive response to you, you may be dealing with a man who has a masochistic need to be dominated and mistreated. If such behavior comes easy and natural for you, it can be exceedingly effective with such men.

97. JUDICIOUSLY MIX TENDERNESS. According to some psychologists, the need for expressing and receiving *tenderness* is even more frustrated and inhibited than the sex drive. Every man needs and appreciates tenderness, and you need to express and receive it. Practice it. You will also find that the man who wants a strong, dominating woman responds best to a judicious counter-point of tenderness and almost brutal domination.

98. PRACTICE GOOD GROOMING. Few men require that you look like Bo Derek. They would just like for you to be attractive.

This means that her hair is neatly styled, clean stylish clothes, sweet breath, clean nails, and frequent bathing. Most men don't like heavy makeup either. Also, try to stay in good shape with a good exercise program and proper diet.

99. STRIVE TO DEVELOP AND LEARN TO PROJECT A QUALITY OF INTENSE FEELING. A passionate interest in life and people, a quality of "excitement: conveyed by one's enthusiasm and intense involvement with life...a rich savoring of the present moment.

100. OPEN YOUR EYES TO THE UNCONVENTIONAL ATTRACTIVENESS AND SEX APPEAL of "plain" man next door! Taste in attractiveness and sex appeal is often a purely subjective quality. Many men whose faces and bodies attract no public attention or enthusiasm may exert a provocative, tantalizing, even aphrodisiacal effect upon you personally...if you open your eyes and find those subtle elements in him only you can appreciate and cherish.

INDEX

Ad writing, 72
Adult education classes, 58, 184
Affirmations, 135, 154, 155, 163, 165
Air Mattress technique, 53
Answering personal ads, 80
Approaching men, 27
Art galleries, 48
Astrology, 143
Autosuggestion, 162

Beaches, 56
Beliefs (misconceived), 130
Body language, 123, 179
Book method, 117
Bowling, 184
Breaking relationships, 37

Card method, 119
Churches, 51
Circulars, 116
Club Med, 100
Computer dating, 66
Conversational skills, 120, 172, 181
Correspondence clubs, 89, 184
Country clubs, 108
Cruises, 104, 105

(Dance only man), 15
Dating referral services, 67, 186
Daytime barflys, 41
Denver men, 170
Department stores, 49

Dressing for nightclubs, 21
Drinkaholic, 14
Drugs, 24

Egotist, 20
Eye closure, 148
Eye contact, 26

Fast-dancing, 29
Fear, 133, 170
Flight attendants, 112
Flirting, 26
Form letters, 77, 81, 85
Friends, 55, 183
Ft. Lauderdale men, 170

Get rich books, 118
Getting ready and psyched up, 22
Golddigger, 16
Grooming, 128, 190

Hair, 128
Health clubs, 52
High and loaded man, 17
Hitchhikers, 39
Horoscopes, 143
Hotels, 42, 186
Houston men, 168
Human potential groups, 51
Hypnotic sleep tapes, 156

Interviews with single men, 33

Jewelry, 128

INDEX

Joe Land Company, 137
Jogging, 47

Looks, 127
Los Angeles men, 168

Magazine personal ads, 90
Magnetic gaze, 166
Mate-seeker, 18
Meeting men in nightclubs, 9
Mental commands, 165
Mental pictures, 150, 154, 161, 163, 165
Mirror technique, 164
Motels, 42

Negative body language, 126
New Orleans men, 170
Newspapers accepting personal ads, 90
Nightclub "Hot Spots," 25
Nightclub Ego-man, 21
Nightclub regulars, 20
Nudists, 61
Nudist publications, 63

Obesity, 128
Obstacles to picking up women, 35
Opening lines, 27, 172, 189
Out With the Boys Men, 15

Parks, 42
Parties, 40
Penpal columns, 87, 184
Personal ads (examples). 73

Personal ads (national publications), 74
Posthypnotic suggestions, 151
Potentials Unlimited, 160
Profiles of nightclub men, 32

Rafting trips, 45,
Relatives, 55, 183, 186
Restaurants, 50
Rich men, 18
Roller rinks, 47, 185

San Diego men, 169
San Francisco men, 169
San Jose men, 169
Seattle men, 169
Seduction routine, 31, 144
Selecting a good nightclub, 10
Self-hypnosis methods, 147
Self-improvement books, 118, 176
Sex, 38, 121
Shy men, 19
Shyness, 129, 180
Shyness tape, 136
Shyness, overcoming, 133
Singles vacations, 100
Singleworld, 102
Skiing, 48
Slow-dancing, 31
Strip joints, 59
Subconscious mind, 135
Subliminal tapes, 136
Supermarkets, 43, 109
Swimming pools, 53
Swimwear, 53, 57

193

INDEX

Teaser, 13
Telepathy, 166
Tennis, 43
Theatre groups, 54, 185
Touching, 31, 122
Tours, 54
Transportation, 50

University extension
 courses, 58

Video dating, 67
Voice, 122, 179
Volunteer activities, 42

Walking, 123, 179
Washington, DC men,
 169
Wealthy men, 107
Windjammer Barefoot
 Cruises, 105
Woman hater, 12
Woman hunter, 16
Women that turn men
 off, 33
Women that turn men
 on, 34
Work, 56, 109, 183

Yacht clubs, 108

100 Ways to Meet and
Attract Men, 171

DO YOU WANT TO ATTRACT MEN? AND DRIVE MEN WILD?

Do you want men to crave your affections morning, noon and night? Are you seeking to improve your "social" life with men ...??? (if you know what I mean).

Would you like men to perceive you as a sexual, sensual beautiful creature of desire? Do you want to be successful with men?

Do you want to have men surround you like bees surround pollen?

Well, I have good news for those few select women who would like to be successful with the opposite sex!

I would like to introduce you to our **Pheromone** attractant spray called, "**ATTRACTANT GOLD.**"

For years, experts have known that men respond to certain natural aromas known as "**pheromones.**" Now, scientists have been able to isolate this natural attractant - and now you can purchase it in spray form exclusively from Gemini.

Order yours today! Send $23 to: Gemini, 11543 Gullwood Dr., Suite 104, Houston, TX 77089

I think she used too much!!

Who wrote the Book Of Love?

WE JUST DID! Our **Friends & Lovers** astrological report profiles show you what's in the stars for your relationship. This personal report is written just for the two of you by a highly-skilled counseling astrologer.

Using your birth dates, we'll calculate your personal horoscopes and compare them. Each report is approximately twenty pages in length, and explores your relationship from several points of view:

How do each of you approach relationships in general? Do you have an easy time becoming intimate? What parts of either personality will help or hinder a relationship, and how are they revealed in the birth chart? Are you sexually, emotionally, and intellectually compatible? Strengths and weaknesses in your relationship...and much, much more.

After exploring these questions for both individuals, the report goes on to see how the two charts interconnect in this unique relationship. How will these two get along? What role does each play here?

The report is calculated just for you (based on your birth dates) and its accuracy can be startling...sometimes it's just too close for comfort!

Let **Friends & Lovers** reveal new insights into non-romantic relationships, too: family, friends, business...anyone you'd like to know more about. ORDER YOUR COMPATIBILITY READING TODAY!

To order, please send your **Birthdate, Birthplace, Time AM/PM? (Must be accurate)** and this **same information** for person #2. Please send $18.95 to: Gemini, 11543 Gullwood Dr., Suite 103, Houston, TX 77089

IMPORTANT! PLEASE INDICATE IF REPORT IS FOR A <u>ROMANTIC</u> OR <u>NON-ROMANTIC</u> RELATIONSHIP!

Other Books to Turn Your Love-Life Around From Gemini Publishing to Meet and Attract the Opposite Sex

_HOW TO FIND THE LOVE OF YOUR LIFE...90 days to a permanent relationship. (#E6501-$10.00)
_50 WAYS TO GET A DATE (#E8757-$6.95)
_PEARLS OF LOVE...How to write love letters and love poems. (#E6504-$10.00)
_SHY PERSONS GUIDE...Cure shyness. (#E9041-$12.95)
_REMARRIAGE REALITY...Guide to remarriage and how to have a happy union. (#E8329-$12.00)
_TOTAL SUCCESS...A-Z guide to success. (#E9389-$14.95)
_THE COMPLETE GUIDE TO MEETING WOMEN...How to meet, attract, and date women. (#M6600-$10.00)
_DO YOU COME HERE OFTEN?...Exciting conversation techniques to meet women. (#M9437-$11.95)
_HOW TO MASSAGE A WOMAN...Book and cassette system for men. (#M9339-$26.95)
_HOW TO MAKE LOVE TO A SINGLE GIRL (#M9559-$14.95)
_SEXUAL CONFIDENCE...Helps men to attract new mates and become better lovers. (#M9230-$14.94)
_SEX POWER...How to seduce women. (#M9365-$11.95)
_HOW TO WIN WITH WOMEN (#M9060-$11.95)
_HOW TO MEET GIRLS WITHOUT REALLY TRYING..... Success techniques on meeting women. (#M9250-$1195)
_TAOIST WAY...Overcome impotence (#M9501-$10.00)
_ATTRACTANT 10...Amazing pheromone chemical spray that attracts women like crazy! (#M9312-$25.00)
_A MAN'S GUIDE TO WOMEN (#M9231-$8.95)
_INNER LOOKS...Guide for men on how to make women notice you. (#M9132-$12.95)
_HOW TO MEET NEW WOMEN...Cassette. (#M9520-$12.95)
_HOW TO PICK UP GIRLS (#M9213-$14.95)
_HOW TO PICK UP WOMEN IN DISCOS (#M9321-$6.95)

Please send me the books I have checked above. I am enclosing $___ (please add $1 for postage and handling). Please send your order to: Gemini Publishing Company, 11543 Gullwood Drive, Suite 105, Houston, TX 77089.

*NOTE: Most titles are not available in the book stores.

Other Books to Turn Your Love-Life Around From Gemini Publishing to Meet and Attract the Opposite Sex

_HOW TO FIND THE LOVE OF YOUR LIFE...90 days to a permanent relationship. (#E6501-$10.00)
_50 WAYS TO GET A DATE (#E8757-$6.95)
_PEARLS OF LOVE...How to write love letters and love poems. (#E6504-$10.00)
_SHY PERSONS GUIDE...Cure shyness. (#E9041-$12.95)
_REMARRIAGE REALITY...Guide to remarriage and how to have a happy union. (#E8329-$12.00)
_TOTAL SUCCESS...A-Z guide to success. (#E9389-$14.95)
_THE COMPLETE GUIDE TO MEETING WOMEN...How to meet, attract, and date women. (#M6600-$10.00)
_DO YOU COME HERE OFTEN?...Exciting conversation techniques to meet women. (#M9437-$11.95)
_HOW TO MASSAGE A WOMAN...Book and cassette system for men. (#M9339-$26.95)
_HOW TO MAKE LOVE TO A SINGLE GIRL (#M9559-$14.95)
_SEXUAL CONFIDENCE...Helps men to attract new mates and become better lovers. (#M9230-$14.94)
_SEX POWER...How to seduce women. (#M9365-$11.95)
_HOW TO WIN WITH WOMEN (#M9060-$11.95)
_HOW TO MEET GIRLS WITHOUT REALLY TRYING..... Success techniques on meeting women. (#M9250-$1195)
_TAOIST WAY...Overcome impotence (#M9501-$10.00)
_ATTRACTANT 10...Amazing pheromone chemical spray that attracts women like crazy! (#M9312-$25.00)
_A MAN'S GUIDE TO WOMEN (#M9231-$8.95)
_INNER LOOKS...Guide for men on how to make women notice you. (#M9132-$12.95)
_HOW TO MEET NEW WOMEN...Cassette. (#M9520-$12.95)
_HOW TO PICK UP GIRLS (#M9213-$14.95)
_HOW TO PICK UP WOMEN IN DISCOS (#M9321-$6.95)

Please send me the books I have checked above. I am enclosing $__ (please add $1 for postage and handling). Please send your order to: Gemini Publishing Company, 11543 Gullwood Drive, Suite 105, Houston, TX 77089.

*NOTE: Most titles are not available in the book stores.